ALL TIME FAVORITE CARD GAMES

By David Galt

W9-ARU-961

Publications International, Ltd.

David Galt is a game designer and consultant who has written extensively on games old and new. His articles have appeared in *Games* magazine, *The Playing Card,* and *Country Collectibles,* and he is also the author of *Card Games for One or Two.* His collection of over 5000 antique games and playing cards includes some of the first in America.

Cover illustration: Guy Wolek

Contents

INTRODUCTION

———◆❖◆———

Can you keep a poker face and play it close to the vest? Well then, here's a not-so-well-kept secret: For the past 600 years, card games have been a great way for people of all ages to have fun!

Card games bring people together to have fun— that's why they've been around so long. Just listen to the words we use, and you'll hear plenty of everyday phrases that stem from the world of card playing.

A veteran Euchre player, for instance, knows the right time to "play a lone hand." "That goes double in spades" is often heard at Pinochle and Gin Rummy tables. Winners at Poker tend to have an "ace in the hole." In Solo, Setback, and Bézique, you must know when to "play your trump card."

Besides encouraging communication, cards teach us a lot. Children can learn about numbers through games like Crazy Eights, Fan Tan, and War. Casino, Cribbage, and Michigan are among the many games that show us the factor of luck. Spades and I Doubt

It require sneaky tactics and a certain amount of guesswork.

Look in the section on solitaire for pastimes with cards to while away an idle moment. You'll find a few games you're not familiar with. We've culled these games from among the many hundreds of solitaire games devised over the past 150 years.

Learn how to play these games and more! The following pages provide instructions for some of the most popular card games of all time. For each game, you will find rules of play, game objective, suggested number of players, card requirements, and scoring rules. Also included are tips to help you formulate a strategy, as well as variations for modifying each game. The rules provided are merely guidelines; you may develop your own variations as well. Finally, the handy glossary should be useful for defining important terms and card-table jargon.

So, if you're looking to deal out some fun, this book is your best bet. You're sure to find a card game to suit any occasion!

2-10-JACK

This is a quick and nifty game, with lots of little agonies and ironies. In pursuing the high-scoring cards, you might instead wind up taking high negative-scoring cards. Its name comes from the high value given to the ♥2-10-J and ♠2-10-J.

Number of players: Two.

Object: To win tricks containing plus cards and to lose tricks containing minus cards.

Count of cards:

♥2, ♥10, ♥J	+10 each
♥A, ♥K, ♥Q	+ 5 each
♠2, ♠10, ♠J	-10 each
♠A, ♠K, ♠Q	- 5 each
♣A, ♣K, ♣Q, ♣J	+ 1 each
♦6	+ 1

The cards: A regular pack of 52 cards is used. Hearts are always trumps; aces are high. The ♠A is called "Speculation." It outranks all the other cards including the ♥A and may be used as trump.

To play: Deal six cards each, one at a time, and place the remaining cards face down as a stock pile.

Nondealer leads to the first trick. You must follow suit if able; otherwise you must trump. If you have no trump, play any card. A trick is won by the higher trump in it or, if it contains no trump, by the higher card of the suit that is led.

If a trump is led, the player holding Speculation has the option of playing it as the highest trump, but is not forced to when it's the only possible trump.

You may also use it to trump a club or diamond trick, and you must do so if it's your only trump. You must play Speculation on a spade lead, if it's your only spade. When leading Speculation, state whether it's a spade or a trump.

After each trick, both players take a new card from the stock, the winner of the trick drawing first. The winner of each trick leads to the next. Continue until all tricks have been taken.

Scoring: Sort the scoring cards in your tricks. Add up the plus cards and subtract the minus cards, and enter your scores. The players' combined scores must be +5, and it's easy to see why—the hearts and

The best way to win the ♥2 (+10) is to void yourself of either clubs or diamonds and trump with it. If you hold Speculation (-5), it's hard to lose it. Your best chance is leading it as a spade when you think your opponent is void and must trump it. Try to use Speculation to capture a plus card.

spades cancel each other out, leaving five cards of +1. The winner is the first player to get to +31.

Tips: 2-10-Jack is not an easy game to control. You have only six cards at once, and you don't know whether you'll be getting useful cards or dangerous cards from the stock. As usual, recalling the cards already played helps a lot, and so does counting trumps.

The 3 through 9 of trumps can be good or bad to have. They can protect your other hearts, but they could wind up trumping high minus cards in spades.

AUCTION PINOCHLE

Although Pinochle developed in Europe out of the popular game Bézique, Auction Pinochle probably was invented by immigrants to America. Its appeal was greatest a century ago, and many believe it to be the all-time-best three-handed card game.

———◆◆◆———

Number of players: Three (or four, with the dealer sitting out each deal).

Object: To score points in melds and in play.

The cards: A 48-card "Pinochle" pack is used. You can put one together from two standard packs by dropping all deuces through 8s. Cards rank—from high to low—A-10-K-Q-J-9.

To play: Deal 15 cards to each player. By tradition, deal in bunches of three, or one bunch of three followed by bunches of four. Deal three cards (not the last three) to a face-down "widow," or "kitty."

The bidding: Starting with the player at dealer's left, each player bids or passes. The lowest bid is 250 points, and bids increase by ten points thereafter. Once you pass you can't reenter the bidding, but bidders can continue raising the auction. The auction is closed once two players have passed. The aim is to score at least as many points as you bid, by scoring for melds and winning tricks (see "Melds in Pinochle" at right).

The player who wins the bid becomes the "bidder." If you are the bidder, turn the three widow cards face up and add them to your hand. It may be clear at this point that your total of melds and cards taken

With this hand, a 300 bid is safe. You have "100 Aces" to meld, plus pinochle (♠Q-♦J), and the "dix," worth 10. In play, your hand should take 150 points. You also have two flushes "open," and if you get a lucky widow, you might have much more to meld. It's probably best not to risk a 400 bid on this type of hand, though.

in play won't reach your bid. You may concede at this point, losing the amount you bid.

Melds in Pinochle:

Flush (A-10-K-Q-J of trumps)	150 points
Royal Marriage (K-Q of trumps)	40 points
Plain Marriage (K-Q of other suit)	20 points
Pinochle (♠Q-♦J)	40 points
100 Aces (♠A-♥A-♣A-♦A)	100 points
80 Kings (♠K-♥K-♣K-♦K)	80 points
60 Queens (♠Q-♥Q-♣Q-♦Q)	60 points
40 Jacks (♠J-♥J-♣J-♦J)	40 points
Dix (pronounced "deece") (9 of trumps)	10 points

(If you declare a flush, you may not also declare the royal marriage it contains.)

Otherwise, table your melds, including cards from the widow, and announce a suit as trumps. If the bidder has already reached or exceeded the value of his bid, play ceases immediately, and he scores the value of his game (see "Scoring").

Your two opponents will temporarily unite in their play against you. In order to reduce your hand back down to 15 cards, choose three unmelded cards to set aside, face down, to add later to the tricks you win. Pick up your melds, and lead any card to the first trick.

The winner of each trick leads to the next. You must always follow suit, and if you cannot follow to a plain suit you must play a trump if possible. When a trump is led, play a higher trump than the previous player if possible. Tricks are taken by the highest card of the suit led or by the highest trump if they are played.

Your trumps. *Opponents' trumps.*

You lead ♥K, so opponents must play ♥10 and ♥A. This allows you to win the remaining trumps when you regain the lead.

When two of the same card, say two ♠As, are played to a trick, the one played first is considered the higher of the two.

When play is over, points are counted in tricks as follows:

Ace	11
10	10
King	4
Queen	3
Jack	2
9	0
Last trick wins 10 points.	

Scoring: If you make your bid, collect points from each opponent according to the following scoring table. If you concede, lose points to each opponent according to the scoring table. If you play the hand and miss your bid, lose double to each opponent for going bête (pronounced "bait").

Bid	Points
250–290	5
300–340	10
350–390	15
400–440	25
450–490	50
500+	100

For bids over 300, spades score double.

Example: You bid 370, and make 405, in spades. You receive 30 points from each opponent. If you had bid 400 and made 405 in spades, you'd win 50 from each. But, if you'd bid 410 and made only 405, you'd go bête in spades and lose 100 points to each opponent.

Tips: Don't count on the widow to provide you the melding help you need. There's just better than a one-in-six chance that one particular card will be there. Even when either of two cards will work, you've only got a one-in-three chance.

In calculating the points you'll lose in play, figure that each opponent may put a high card on your losing tricks.

As defenders, remember the cards you've seen the bidder meld that you can beat. These are cards you should be sure to win. Occasionally the bidder will have even more cards of that suit in his hand, as a "side suit" in addition to trumps.

Variations: Bidding practices have their own traditions. In one, after two passes the dealer must take with a bid of at least 250. In another, the dealer passes out the hand, or opens it at 290 (but not at 250) or at 320 or higher. A third treatment requires the first hand to start at 300, and it is allowed to throw the hand in for the minimum-stake loss.

In *Four-Handed Partnership Pinochle,* partners sit facing each other. Deal 12 cards each, three at a time. Turn up the last card as trumps. If it's a 9, dealer scores 10 points. Otherwise, whoever first has a 9 may replace it with the trump upcard. Players in turn table their melds, which are recorded. Cards are picked up, and the player at dealer's left begins by leading any card. Partners pool their tricks taken, and at the end of play count their points (last trick counts 10). The deal rotates. Game is played to 1000 points.

AUCTION PITCH

This widely played game, also known as High-Low-Johnny or Setback, descends from seventeenth-century England's All-Fours. Its contemporary cousins include Seven-Up, Pedro, Cinch, and California Jack.

———◆•✕•◆———

Number of players: Two.

Object: To score points by winning cards in tricks. The four points to be won are the hand holding high trump for the deal, the hand holding low trump for the deal, the trick taking the jack of trump, and "game"—the high card-count total in tricks taken.

The cards: A regular pack of 52 cards is used. Aces are high; however, 10s are the highest-scoring cards (see "Scoring").

To play: Deal six cards to each player, three at a time. The rest of the cards are not needed.

Starting with nondealer, each player bids once for the right to choose the trump suit. The possible bids are—from weakest to strongest—one, two, three, and four. Dealer, in order to bid, must outbid non-dealer, but either one may "pass" (not bid). If both players happen to pass, throw the cards in and then deal a new hand.

High bidder designates the trump suit by leading a card of that suit to the first trick. This is the "pitch." You must follow suit if a trump card is led. If another suit is led you may play a trump even if you are able to follow suit. You may not discard, however, if you are able to follow suit. A trick is won by the higher trump in it or, if the trick contains no trump, by the higher card. The winner of each trick leads to the next.

Scoring: When the six tricks have been played, score each hand.

High trump	1
Low trump	1
Jack of trumps	1
Game (high card-count total)	1
Each ace	4
Each king	3
Each queen	2
Each 10	10

The points for high and low trump card are each awarded to the player whose hand contained the card, not the player who took the card in a trick.

The point for jack of trumps (if the card was present) goes to the player who took it in a trick. Whoever has taken the higher card count in tricks earns 1 point for game (in case of tie, neither wins this point).

Each player scores the number of points earned on the deal. The bidder must score at least the number bid or else is "set back" (loses) that amount. The first player to reach 11 wins (or you may agree to another number, for example 7, 13, or 21).

Tips: When you hold three or more trumps, it's unlikely that opponent has more than two. It's often wise to "draw" opponent's trumps by continuing to lead them. Remember, opponent is free to play a trump card instead of following suit.

Don't bid four without seeing the jack of trumps in your hand.

BÉZIQUE

Bézique, the forerunner of Pinochle, was invented in the early 1800s in Sweden. By the 1850s, it was a hit all across Europe, and it soon arrived in America. It's still widely enjoyed in Britain, where score is kept with individual Bézique "markers."

Number of players: Two.

Object: To score points by melding and by taking tricks containing aces and 10s (called "brisques").

The cards: Two sets of 32 cards, consisting of aces through 7s, are shuffled together into one 64-card deck. Cards rank—from high to low—A-10-K-Q-J-9-8-7.

To play: Deal eight cards to each player (in groups of three, two, and three), and then turn up a card to designate trumps. Place that card face up and so that it is slightly sticking out from under the draw pile. If the trump upcard is a 7, dealer scores 10 points immediately.

Melds are worth the following amount of points:

Trump marriage (K-Q)	40 points
Non-trump marriage (K-Q in same suit)	20 points
Trump flush (A-10-K-Q-J)	250 points
Bézique (♠Q + ◆J)	40 points
Double Bézique (♠Q + ◆J + ♠Q + ◆J)	500 points
♥A-◆A-♠A-♣A	100 points
♥K-◆K-♠K-♣K	80 points
♥Q-◆Q-♠Q-♣Q	60 points
♥J-◆J-♠J-♣J	40 points
7 of trumps (each)	10 points

Nondealer starts play by leading any card. At this stage of play, and as long as there remain cards to draw, you are not obliged to follow suit, but may play any of your cards.

The highest trump in a trick wins it, or, if there is no trump card, the highest card of the suit led wins it. When two identical cards contend for the same trick (for example, two ♥10s), the first one played wins the trick.

The winner of each trick scores 10 points for each ace or 10 (brisque) it contains, and may also table any one meld. (You may tally the 10 points for a 7 of trumps along with another meld, and if you meld

Hearts are trumps. The ♥K and ♥Q form a 40-point mar-
riage. On a later turn, if you are able to add the ♥A-♥10-♥J,
you can score another 250 points for the trump flush. Remem-
ber that you can make only one meld per turn, and only if
you've just won a trick.

the first 7 of trumps you may also trade it for the
trump upcard.) Tally all points as you score them.

Both players take a new card from the stock, with
the winner of the previous trick drawing first and
then leading to the next trick.

Melded cards stay on the table until the stock is
used up, but you may still play them on tricks. A
card you meld one time can be used again, but only
in a different meld. For example: ♣Q melds with
♣K in a marriage and can also meld later for 60
points with ♥Q-♦Q-♠Q. But it can't meld with a
second ♣K—a completely new pair is needed to
score the second marriage.

When only the upcard and one draw card remain,
the upcard goes to the trick-loser. Put your remain-

Example of early play: You're dealt ♦Q, ♦7, ♥J, ♥J, ♣A, ♠A, ♠10, ♠Q, with the ♦K upcard. Your first plan is to win a trick in order to exchange your ♦7 for the ♦K, letting you immediately meld a 40-point trump marriage (♦K-♦Q). You don't want to waste the ♣A, a good melding card, to try to take an early trick. You might try the ♠10, but a less risky choice is one of your ♥Js, which will likely win the trick if your opponent doesn't have a ♥10.

ing melded cards back in your hand, with the winner of the previous trick taking the last draw card and leading to the next trick. In the play of the final eight cards, however, each player must follow suit and also must win a trick whenever possible. Whoever wins the final trick scores an extra 10 points.

Scoring: The first player to accumulate 1000 points—or any other agreed upon sum—wins.

Tips: The play in Bézique has 32 tricks, most of which occur when your opponent can legally trump any ace or 10 you lead. Therefore, you should save your 10s to win lower cards when your opponent

Your hand.   *Opponent's hand.*

The last eight tricks of a Bézique hand. Here, diamonds are trumps and it's your lead. If you lead ♥10, followed by ♠J and ♠8, you'll win the brisques for the ♥10s and should also score 10 for last trick with a high trump. See what happens if you start with the ♣K or ♣Q: You'll lose the lead before playing your ♥10, and then your opponent can win both ♥10 brisques and the last trick!

leads. Meanwhile, there's usually a difficult suit for your opponent to win tricks in. Even if you lead low cards of that suit, it may cause discomfort: Players want to hold on to melding cards (aces, kings, queens, the 10 and jack of trumps, and ♠Q and ♦J for a possible 500-point double bézique). Yet each player can hold just eight cards!

If you have a big meld near the end of the game—for example, ♠Q-♠Q-♦J-♦J—you may not have time to meld it in two stages to score an extra 40 points. Your opponent may see through that plan and prevent you from winning a second trick, and the additional 500 points.

Variations: *Rubicon Bézique,* using 128 cards (a double Bézique pack), emphasizes melding. Deal nine cards each. Trumps are fixed by the first marriage melded instead of by turning a trump card up, and new melds include triple bézique (1500 points), quadruple bézique (4500 points), and back door (non-trump A-10-K-Q-J), which counts 150 points.

Every deal is scored independently. The last trick counts 50. No one bothers with brisques, unless the loser needs the brisque points to get over 1000 points and so prevent being rubiconned. The winner of a rubicon game scores a 1000-point bonus instead of 500, gets 320 points for brisques, and gets all of opponent's other points too!

If you're dealt a "carte blanche" (no picture cards), show it and score 50 points, and score 50 more after each draw until you do get a picture card!

You can remake a meld merely by replacing a played melded card!

CANASTA

Canasta—the Spanish word for basket—evolved in Uruguay and spread across Latin America in the 1940s. In 1950, the game swept like wildfire across the United States. Now, nearly a half-century later, Canasta may do so once again.

Number of players: Four, in partnerships seated across the table.

Object: To score points by melding, with the goal of scoring two canastas and then "going out."

The cards: Two regular packs of 52 cards plus their four jokers are used. Jokers and deuces are wild.

Melding: Melds must consist of at least three cards, all of the same rank. All melds are placed face up on the table, and partners build up their melds together to form "canastas"—seven-card bonus melds. All jokers and deuces are wild and can be used in melds as any desired rank except 3s. A canasta must consist of at least four natural cards but may contain any number of wild cards.

The treys: Red 3s are bonus cards worth 100 points each, but they are not used in play. You should lay down a red 3 as soon as you can. If your side scores all four red 3s, the bonus for them doubles to 800 points.

Black 3s are used in play, but are meldable only when "going out." Otherwise, they function as stopper cards (see "Freezing the pack").

To play: Deal 11 cards to each player, one at a time, turning over an upcard that starts a discard pile called the "pack." The remainder of the cards form the stock. Note: If the upcard is a wild card or a red 3, turn another card up on top of it, and see "Freezing the pack."

The player at dealer's left goes first, with play passing in clockwise rotation until the hand is over. At your turn, even on the first round of play, you may "take the pack" with an appropriate hand of cards

15 points   90 points   40 points

(see "Taking the pack"), but your usual turn consists of drawing one card and then discarding one card.

Initial melds: The first player to meld for a side must table at least 50 points of meld. All cards have point values for melding.

Joker	50 points
Deuce	20 points
Ace	20 points
King through 8	10 points
7 through 4	5 points
Black 3s	5 points

To calculate the value of a meld, simply add up the value of the cards it contains. Note that a three-card (or longer) meld must have at least two natural cards.

The initial melding requirement increases along the way as detailed in the table below:

Score at the beginning of new deal	Minimum initial meld
Less than 0	15 points
0–1495	50 points
1500–2995	90 points
3000 or more	120 points

Taking the pack: You are allowed to take the pack—the entire current pile of discards—as long as

You don't have to "take the pack" to make an initial meld, but it gives you more cards to play with. Wait until there are enough cards (around 10 or 12) in the pack to take it, so you will have more cards in your hand. In this case, taking the upcard gives you enough for a 60-point meld: ♥J-♦J-♣J + ♠5-♥5-♣2.

you can meld the top discard and meet the following conditions. If your side hasn't melded yet, you'll need two natural cards to meld with the upcard, and you must meet the minimum meld required for your side (without using any other cards in the pack). If your side has melded already, then one natural card with one wild card will do, and you may even take the pack if your opponent's discard can go in one of your melds.

Also, once your side has met its initial meld, you may use the pack to form new melds or add to your melds to form canastas, as you wish. Any cards you don't meld become part of your hand.

Once a meld is on the table, either partner may play off it. When a meld contains seven or more cards, it

Displaying a red card on top of the meld denotes a natural canasta (500 points, no wild cards), while a black card—if available—signals a mixed canasta (300 points, one to three wild cards).

becomes a canasta. It is squared into a pile and a red card is placed on top if it consists of all natural cards (a natural canasta). A black card is placed on top if it contains any wild cards or 3s (a mixed canasta). If any wild cards are later added to a "red" canasta, it becomes a "black" canasta, and its value changes accordingly.

Freezing the pack: Freezing the pack makes it difficult for any player to take the pack. To freeze the pack, discard a wild card sideways across the discards. The next player can't take the pack as long as a wild card remains. To pick up a frozen pack, you'll need a natural pair in your hand. This rule applies to all players, regardless of who froze the pack initially.

A black 3 freezes the pack momentarily, except in the unlikely event that a player with two black 3s can "go out" while taking the pack. That would require using every card taken in the pack. (Note: Wild cards may not meld with black 3s.)

A turn is completed by the player discarding one card face up on the pack.

Going out: You "go out" (sometimes called going "rummy") if you meld all the cards in your hand. However, in order to go out, your side has to have at least one canasta, and in most games you need one card left over to discard. Play ceases at this point, and the score for the hand is tallied.

Before going out, you are allowed to ask your partner "May I go out?" but you must abide by the answer. Should no one go rummy, the hand ends when the stock is gone and the pack can't be taken.

Scoring: Total the value of all melded cards and add bonuses for going rummy (100), natural canastas (500), mixed canastas (300), and red 3s (100 each, but 800 for all four). Subtract the total of cards left in each player's hand (red 3s count -200 points), and tally each team's score. Game is to 5000 points.

Tip: When taking the pack, don't meld everything in it immediately. It is wise to keep some cards so that you'll have natural pairs to take a frozen pack.

CASINO

Casino has descended to us directly from Scopa, the old Italian game. Widely enjoyed as a two- or three-handed game, Casino is also entertaining for four players—either as partners or "cutthroat" style.

Number of players: Two to four.

Object: To score points by winning cards in play by matching, combining, and building.

The cards: A regular pack of 52 cards is used.

To play: Deal four cards face down to each player and four to the table face up. Keep the remaining cards at hand to deal the following rounds. The player at dealer's left plays the first card of each round, with play continuing in clockwise order. When all players have played their four cards, the same dealer deals four more cards to each player. Cards are dealt to the table only in the first round, however.

At your turn, you might simply place a card on the table (see "Trailing"). However, there are several

A Casino hand (top) and table layout (bottom).

ways to take cards—or to try to take them: by
matching, by combining, by building, and by taking
another player's build.

You can combine the card you play with the cards
on the table in many possible ways. Suits do not
matter.

Matching: If your card matches the rank of a card
on the table, you can take the pair immediately,
placing them in your own stack face down in front
of you. In the illustrated hand, you can take the ♥Q
with the ♣Q, or you can take the ♠7 with the ♦7.
Face cards match in pairs only—when two kings are
on the table and you hold one king in your hand,

you capture only one of the kings. However, if three kings are dealt to the table, whoever has the fourth king takes them all. Plain cards can match in greater numbers.

Combining: If your card equals the combined sum of two or more cards on the table, you can take the cards immediately. In the deal shown, you may combine the ♣6 and ♣2 and take them away with the ♦8.

Building: If at least one card on the table plus the card you play totals another card in your hand, announce this build number and pile the build-cards together. In the example shown on page 31, play the ♠A onto the ♠7, and say "Building 8s." You may also put the ♣6 and ♣2 into this build, making it a "multiple build." On your next turn—if no one's taken your build—you can pick it up with your ♦8. (And, if you have no other build or capture, you must.) At your turn, you can take an opponent's build when you have the right card, and, of course, an opponent can take yours as well.

Occasionally, with the right holding, you can increase an opponent's build. With a deuce and a 10, play the deuce on top of a simple 8-build and announce "Building 10s." Multiple builds, by the way, can't be built up to a higher number.

Trailing: If you have nothing else to do on your turn, you must trail a card—place it on the table without building it onto another card. You cannot do this if you have made a build that's still on the table.

When dealing the last round, call "Last" to alert the other players. Whoever takes the final cards on the last round also wins any untaken cards remaining at the end.

Scoring: Players count their cards and note the cards with extra value. Each deal has 11 points.

♦10 (Big Casino)	2 points
♠2 (Little Casino)	1 point
Each ace	1 point
"Spades" (Player who takes the most spades)	1 point
"Cards" (Player who takes the most cards)	3 points

When there's a tie for "cards" in a two-player game, neither scores for it. In a three-handed game, those tied score 2 points each; in larger games, those tied score 1 point each.

Play to 21 points, or to any other agreed number.

Tips: The more players in a game, the riskier it is to build. In a four-handed game, someone is likely to take a build made early in the round, so try to delay your build, if possible.

The fewer players in a game, the more you can control the action. It will help to know which key cards remain—10s, aces, and other high building cards. A skilled player in a two-handed game knows which cards have been played and which cards are left for the final round.

Variations: In *Scoops,* 1 point is scored for a "scoop"—a play that clears the table. Signify scoops by facing one card up for each.

Continuous Casino: Deal as in regular Casino, but leave the stock of undealt cards in everybody's reach. In this game, take a new card after each play. No further rounds of cards are dealt. (This method can accommodate five players.)

Partnership Casino: Teammates sit across from each other, keeping winnings together and trying, within the rules, to help each other.

CONCENTRATION

*The most appropriately named game of all time!
"Concentration" is what you'll need to win this game.
Since children sometimes are better at this game than
adults are, it can be an enjoyable pastime for the
entire family.*

———◆◆◆———

Number of players: Two or more.

Object: To gather in the most cards by matching
them in pairs.

The cards: A regular pack of 52 cards is used.

To play: You'll need a large surface area. Deal the
whole deck out, card by card, face down. It doesn't
matter if the cards are in neat rows or in a haphaz-
ard arrangement.

By tradition, the youngest player goes first. Each
turn consists of turning up one card and then another, taking care to keep them in place. When the
two cards match in rank, put them in your winnings
pile and continue your turn, revealing two new
cards.

These two cards don't match, but remember where they are for later play!

However, when the cards you turn over are of different rank, your turn ends. Return them to their places, face down. Try to concentrate on remembering where each card lies, as you may still pair one or the other later.

Scoring: When the cards have all been matched, record the number of cards you've taken. Whoever has the most cards after three games wins.

Tip: Concentration rewards visual recall, and some people are just better at this than others. This tip can help you keep pace: Say you've just seen an-

other player turn the ♥5 and you suspect you remember the location of a 5 seen earlier. When your
turn comes, go first for the earlier 5, not for the ♥5.
When you're right, all you have to do is grab the ♥5
(but don't forget where it is). This way, if the first
card you turn over is not a 5, you've still got a
chance to find a match for it!

Variations: With a very young crowd of players,
you may want to omit some cards for a smaller
layout. For example, you may wish to leave out all
aces, 3s, 5s, 7s, and 9s.

For a more advanced crowd, play Moving Concentration: You may return pairs that don't match to
new spots in the layout!

COON CAN

A game that appears to have originated down South, "Coon Can" comes from the Spanish ¿con quien? (meaning "with whom?"). Also known as Conquian, it is one of the few rummy games that has lasted over a century. Perhaps its colorful lingo contributes to its long-term appeal.

Number of players: Two.

Object: To "go coon can," that is to meld all your cards, plus an extra card you pick from the draw or discard pile. As in most rummy games, melds must be at least three cards long.

The cards: A 40-card pack (akin to a Spanish pack), with all 10s, 9s, and 8s removed, is used. This leaves the jack and 7 in sequence. Aces are low.

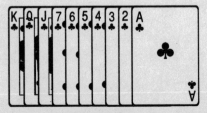

Rank order in Coon Can.

Short spreads.   *Long spreads.*

Melding: Melds in Coon Can must have at least three cards and are left on the table.

To play: Deal ten cards each and leave the rest face down as a draw pile. Nondealer begins by plucking (turning up) and showing the top card from stock. You cannot add a plucked card to your hand, so if this card is not used in a meld, it must be discarded. Each player in turn must either take the top discard and meld it, or turn up the top card from stock and add it to a spread or discard it.

In Coon Can, you can move cards from one meld to another (switch) as long as you leave only legal spreads.

COON CAN'S TERMINOLOGY:

Hit (noun). A card laid off on a meld.

Hit (verb). To lay a card off on a meld.

Hole. A hand you can't go coon can with.

Long spread. Suit sequence meld.

Pluck. To pick a card from stock.

Short spread. Meld of the same rank.

Sleep it. To purposely overlook a play.

Switch. To move a card from one meld to another.

During one turn, you may hit your own spreads with any number of cards, but when you hit your opponent's spread, that's considered your discard. Actually, when your spread is hit by your opponent, you have 11 cards. You must discard from your hand instead of plucking a new card!

You may shift your own melds around to create new melds as long as you leave only valid melds behind.

If you go coon can (have 11 cards in spreads), the game ends and you win the agreed stake. Occasionally, no one goes coon can—a "tab game"—and the stake for it is added to the next game.

Forcing: Opponent shows these two spreads. When you "hit" with ♠Q, it forces the discard of one of the two concealed cards.

Tips: A good amount of skill is involved in hitting your opponent with the intent of forcing a discard from his hand. This discard may be a card you can use, or it may spoil your adversary's plans. Also, you may be able to force your opponent into a "hole"—a hand that can't go coon can. For instance, a hand that's a ten-card-long spread (a spread of an entire suit, for example) can't go coon can, since an eleventh card is required.

Sleeping it: Discarding a card that could match one's own spread may often be a good strategy, but it can be stopped. When you see your opponent "sleeping it," you may force your opponent to hit with it instead, forcing a further discard.

Variations: People who are uncomfortable with placing a 7 and jack in sequence may instead use a 40-card pack, aces through 10s, removing all face cards.

Some games permit players to pluck a card just "on speculation," rather than requiring it to be immediately melded or added to a spread.

CRAZY EIGHTS

Eights are wild and so is the action in this fast-paced game the whole family can play. An easy-to-learn game that calls for a lot of luck, Crazy Eights is a very good game to play with kids.

———◆·◆·◆———

Number of players: Two to six. Even more can play, but the more players, the longer each person has to wait between turns.

Object: To be the first player to get rid of all your cards.

The cards: A regular pack of 52 cards is used, but with four or more players you might want to use two packs.

To play: Deal seven cards to each player, turn one card up to start a discard pile, and leave the rest of the cards next to the pile as a draw stack. The player at dealer's left begins by covering the upcard with a matching card—one that's either the same suit or same rank. For example, if the starter is ◆7, any diamond or any 7 can be played. Whenever you can't match, draw cards until you find a match.

It's your turn to match the ♥4. Choose ♣4, ♥Q, or ♥9. Save the wild card (♦8) for when you really need it!

All 8s are wild and can be played at any time. Call the 8 any suit; the next player must match it. (Don't specify a rank.)

Play rotates to the left, as each player matches the top card, and continues until one player has no cards left. If you run out of draw cards along the way, simply turn over the discard pile, shuffle well, and use it for a new face-down draw pile.

Scoring: Whoever goes out scores the point total of cards left in everyone else's hands. Each 8 counts 50, face cards count 10, and all others count their pip value (face value; ace = 1). The game usually ends after an agreed time limit or number of deals.

Tips: When you have many cards of one suit, others may find that suit hard to match. Remember, in a game with several players, your play affects the next player most.

Don't get caught holding wild cards at the end of play, since they count a whopping 50 points each!

Variations: In *No-Shuffle Crazy Eights,* once the stock is gone, pass when you have no play. Sometimes a "blocked" game results, where no one can match the top discard and no one has an 8. When this occurs, players count their points, and whoever has the lowest total wins the difference in hand-count from each other player.

Double Crazy Eights: Turn the upcard sideways so that two piles can fit on it. As play goes on, you may choose which pile to play on. You may still play an 8 anytime, but you must match it next by its own suit.

CRIBBAGE

This quietly appealing game, which has been played for more than 350 years, is in a class by itself. It may take you a few moments to learn, but once you pick it up you'll begin to admire its many chances for thought and strategy. Since scoring occurs at nearly every moment, a cribbage board is very useful for scoring, or "pegging."

Number of players: Two to four. The two-handed game will be described first.

Object: To score points for certain card combinations and be the first to peg 121 points (or 61; whatever is agreed upon).

The cards: A regular pack of 52 cards is used. Each card has a point value equal to its rank. Aces are low and count 1. Face cards count 10.

To play: Deal six cards to each player. Both players then select two cards to discard for a face-down, four-card "crib" belonging to the dealer. The goal in discarding is to retain a hand of four cards that will form scoring combinations.

Nondealer selects ♥8, ♦K to discard for the crib. *Dealer selects ♠5, ♠J to discard for the crib.*

The dealer lays the crib aside without looking at it, and it is not used until after the play.

Scoring combinations:

Fifteen: any combination of cards totaling exactly 15	2 points
Pair: two cards of the same rank	2 points
Triplet: three cards of the same rank	6 points
Quartet: four cards of the same rank	12 points
Sequence: three or more cards in a row, any suit	1 point per card
Flush: any four cards of the same suit	1 point per card
His Nobs: jack of the starter's suit, in hand	1 point

It should be noted that flushes and His Nobs don't score during play.

Next, nondealer cuts the pack and dealer turns up the top card (the "start" or "starter"). If the start is a jack, dealer scores 2 points for "His Nobs." The starter card is not used in play. The remaining cards form the stock, which is not used in this hand.

Nondealer now plays one card face up, calling out its value. Dealer does the same, calling the total of the two cards played. Continue in this way as long as the count doesn't exceed 31. Keep cards in two separate piles—one for dealer's cards, one for non-dealer's cards. When you can't play without exceeding 31, say "Go," which instructs your opponent to continue play without going past 31, as opponent pegs 1 for your "go." If opponent is able to reach 31 exactly after your "go," he pegs 2 instead of 1 (1 for 31, 1 for "go"). When both players are unable to play, a new count is begun by the player who didn't make the last play. Playing the last card of all counts 1 point.

Pegging for melds made in play: Cards must be played consecutively within one 31-count to score. In addition to the scoring for "go," 31, and the last card, combinations made during play also score points. If your play makes the count 15, score 2. If you match the rank of the card played by opponent, score 2 for the pair. Three cards of the same rank are worth 6 points, and the fourth one scores 12. Se-

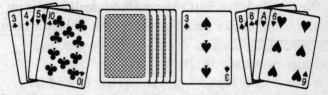

Nondealer starts by saying "Three." Dealer plays the ♣8 and says "11." Nondealer plays ♦4 and says "15 for 2" while pegging 2. This is followed by "23," "28," "29," and "go." Dealer also cannot play under 31 but pegs 1 for nondealer's "go." Nondealer begins the new count by playing the ♣10 and calling "Ten." "Sixteen and last," says dealer, pegging 1.

quences also count, and the cards don't have to be in exact order. For example, 3-6-4-5 scores 4 points for the last player, and if the next player follows with a deuce, that sequence is worth 5 points. A flush (series of cards of the same suit) does not score in play; it scores only when scoring the hand.

Scoring the hands: After you've played out the cards, nondealer's hand is counted and pegged (see "Scoring combinations"), followed by dealer's hand, and then dealer's crib. This order is important because if at any point either player reaches 121 (or 61), the game is immediately ended. The start card is scored as a fifth card in each hand.

In the illustrated hand (*above*), nondealer pegs 12: two sequences (3-4-5, 3-4-5), one pair (3s), and two

15s (5-10, 3-3-4-5). Dealer pegs 6: two 15s (8-6-A, 8-6-A) and a pair (8s). By custom, nondealer now separates the start card, gathers in the rest, and dealer pegs the crib. In this case, (see page 47) it's worth 5: two 15s (5-J, 5-K) and His Nobs (♠J).

At the end of each hand, all the cards (from dealer's hand, nondealer's hand, crib, and stock) are gathered and shuffled together to form a fresh pack of 52 for the next hand. Nondealer from last hand becomes dealer for new hand.

Pegging out: As soon as you peg to 121 (or to 61, as agreed), the game ends, no matter when this occurs. If the loser fails to score at least 61 points in a game of 121, he is "skunked," or "lurched," and the winner scores for a double game.

The board has 30 holes in each of the long rows, marked off in groups of five. Each player gets two pegs. In the beginning, the four pegs sit at the start end of the board. The pegs move up the outside and down the inside back to the start, for a total of 61 points. The usual game is two trips, or 121 points. The two pegs are used alternately, with the back peg leap-frogging over the front peg.

Tips: In play, start with a card under 5 so that the next player can't peg a quick 2 points for 15. Hold back your low cards to help score for "go" or 31. Also, keep an eye open for surprise sequences. For instance, if the first cards are a 6 and a 2, and a 3, 4, and 5 are the next cards (in any order), peg 5 points!

Keep in mind who gets the crib when you contribute to it. Pairs or 5s put in your own crib can be better than holding them, but give your opponent high and low cards—say a queen and a 2. Also, since you discard for the crib right away, consider how the cards you keep might fit with various start cards.

Near the end of the game, desperate strategies may be called for. For example, if you are dealer and both you and your opponent need a few points to win, you'll need to peg out in play, since your opponent's hand scores ahead of yours. Therefore, keep cards that can score points in play—forget about making a high-scoring hand.

Variations: If your opponent fails to peg for a score, call "Muggins" and peg the points yourself. Friendly games often omit this rule.

Cribbage for Three: Each player competes independently. If you're using a cribbage board, two players will have to peg up and down a single line of pegging-holes.

Deal five cards to each player, and one card to the crib. Each player then chooses one card to add to the crib. For the start card, dealer offers either adversary the cut. Player at dealer's left then starts play, which proceeds clockwise. "Go" still scores 1 point; and if two players in succession say "go" it still pegs 1. (With three players, you may receive a point for "go" and later in the same count say "go" yourself.)

Cribbage for Four: Although this can be played "cutthroat" style—each player on his or her own—more commonly it's a partnership game, played with the partners facing each other.

Deal five cards to each player. Each player then donates one card to the crib. Only one player pegs for each side, with the cribbage board placed between these two players. Partners may, however, point out counts or melds to each other.

DEMON

This is a solitaire game played by many people at once, with everybody building on common piles. Action and noise can reach high levels, so you may need to keep a whistle handy!

———◆◆◆———

Number of players: Two to eight.

Object: To play out more cards than any other player.

The cards: A regular pack of 52 cards is used per player. Each pack of cards should have a different back design.

To play: Each player deals a layout for the solitaire widely known as "Klondike" (called "Canfield" in England). Refer to the diagram on page 54 for the proper layout.

Wait for all players to complete their layouts. At a signal, turn over three cards from stock to start your "waste heaps," and begin making plays. Once the game is underway, play at your own pace.

To achieve this layout, first deal a row of seven cards with the leftmost one face up and the rest face down. On top of the face-down cards, deal another row, with the leftmost of these face up. Keep doing this until you have seven piles, ranging from one card on the left to seven cards on the right, with the top cards face up. The remainder of the cards form the stock.

There are several moves available to you. You should release your aces into the center of the table as soon as possible, where any player can build them up in sequence by suit, ending with the king. These piles are called "foundation piles."

You can build downward sequences on the cards in your layout, in alternating suit color only. For example, the ♥10 can be moved upon the ♣J, but not on the ◆J. Play cards onto the center foundation piles as available. Note that everyone can play onto each foundation pile, but each player can only build onto his own layout.

When you move a card from its pile, turn up the card beneath. Occasionally a pile empties, opening

up a vacancy. You can fill this only with a king or
with a sequence headed by a king.

The topmost card of your waste heap is always
available for play, as is any single card on a pile, and
also the topmost (lowest) card of a sequence.

In the illustrated hand *(left),* move the ♦8 onto the
♠9, then move both to the ♥10, and move these to
the ♣J. All of these end up on the ♥Q! What a start!
You're now left with one empty pile and three new
cards to turn up.

When you've gone through the stock, three cards at
a time, turn your waste heap over to make a new
stock. You can continue to do this as often as you
like. At some point you may run out of plays, but as
other players develop their layouts, your cards may
become eligible to play in the center, and you may
find several more plays.

The game ends when one player's cards have all
been played into the middle foundation piles. That
player shouts "Demon," and all further play ceases.
The cards on the foundation piles are then sorted
out to return to each respective player. (The game is
also considered complete when no player can find a
play.)

Scoring: A player going out scores 52 points plus a 10-point bonus, and everyone else gets 1 point per card in the foundation piles. One player keeps a tally for everyone, and at the end of an agreed upon number of deals the winner is the one with the highest total score.

Note: Not infrequently, two players will attempt to play the same card on the same foundation pile. Whoever's card is at the bottom is deemed to have gotten there first.

Tips: Fast action is a key to winning, so set yourself up to make quick consecutive plays to the foundation piles.

Keep the center orderly by turning over the foundation piles that have been completely built up to king.

To keep the game alive, you may point out plays to another player.

Variation: Play solitaires other than Klondike that offer common scoring piles for all players.

EUCHRE

Euchre is thought to have descended directly from Triomphe, an immensely popular sixteenth-century game. A hundred years ago in America, Euchre had plenty of devotees and was even considered our national game!

Number of players: Four, with partners seated facing each other. Euchre may also be played by two or three players.

Object: To score points by winning at least three of five tricks.

The cards: A 32-card pack, aces through 7s for each suit, is used. All 2s through 6s are discarded before

Rank of cards in trumps, with clubs as the trump suit.

play. Cards rank as follows: A-K-Q-J-10-9-8-7, except in trumps, where the jack (called the "right bower") is high, and the other jack of the same color (the "left bower") is the second highest trump.

To play: Deal five cards to each player, in bunches of two and three, or three and two, and turn up the next card to propose a trump suit. If that suit becomes the trump suit, the upcard replaces another in dealer's hand. By custom, it stays on the table, while the card it replaces is put beneath the remaining undealt cards.

Determining the trump suit: Starting at dealer's left, each player has a chance to accept or pass the suit turned as trumps. To accept, an opponent of the dealer says "I order it up," dealer's partner says "I assist," and dealer accepts by discarding. Any player may pass.

On balance, to "accept" you should judge your side at least a two-to-one favorite, since you win only 1 point when you succeed (unless you score a march), but lose 2 points when you fail (see "Scoring").

If all four players pass, dealer places the upcard under the pack of undealt cards, and another round follows, to find a trump suit. Starting with the player at dealer's left, each may pass until one player names a trump suit other than the suit first turned up. If all players again pass, throw the cards in and shuffle for a new deal.

When accepting or naming a trump suit, you may also declare at that time to "play alone." Your partner's hand is put aside, and you play against both opponents.

The player at dealer's left usually leads to the first trick, but when you play a lone hand, the defender at your left leads first.

On each trick, follow to the suit of the card led if possible. Otherwise, play any card. Each trick is won by the highest card of the suit led, except a trick containing at least one trump, which is won by the highest trump played. Note that the ♥J is not considered a heart when diamonds are trumps!

Scoring:

Declaring side wins three or four tricks	1 point
Declaring side wins five tricks (a "march")	2 points
If "lone hand" wins	4 points
Declaring side "euchred" (wins fewer than three tricks), opponents score	2 points

Game is played to a predetermined amount of points, usually 5, 7, or 10.

Tips: The trump suit has nine cards, but there are only seven cards in the other suit of the same color. The two remaining suits have eight cards each. Since each deal leaves out about a third of the deck, on average only five or six cards of each suit are in play. If you have three cards in the trump suit and your partner can take a trick, you are likely to win the majority of tricks.

When you have three practically certain winning cards in your hand and chances of winning the other cards, it may be wise to play alone. Your non-trump cards, even if not clear winners, may take tricks anyway: Your opponents have only ten cards between them, and may fail to hold on to the right cards!

Don't forget that if the upcard is accepted as trumps, it becomes part of the dealer's hand. This may influence your decision to accept that suit as trumps for your side.

The "game" score may also influence your decision to pass, accept, or play alone. If you have a large lead, it may be a good risk to venture a questionable acceptance of the trump suit if you fear an opponent may score a "march" (4 points) in a different suit. Even if you're euchred, opponent scores only 2 points.

Variations: *Two-Handed Euchre* is generally played with a 24-card pack, omitting 7s and 8s as well. Score for a "march" is 2 points, and the option to declare a lone hand does not exist.

Three-Handed Euchre: The player who makes trumps plays against the other two, who temporarily unite as partners.

The scoring is as follows:

Maker of trump suit wins three or four tricks	1 point
Maker of trump suit wins five tricks (a "march")	3 points
Maker of trump suit is euchred, each opponent wins	2 points

Railroad Euchre: A joker is added as the highest trump, regardless of suit.

FAN TAN

Don't confuse Fan Tan—also known as Card Dominoes, Sevens, and Parliament—with "Chinese Fan Tan," an unrelated gambling game.

Number of players: Three to eight, but the game is best when four play.

Object: To be the first to play off all your cards.

The cards: A regular pack of 52 cards is used. Aces are low.

A Fan Tan game in progress after several plays.

To play: Give each player an equal supply of chips; you'll need a bowl or a dish to collect them in. Deal one card at a time to each player, until the whole pack is dealt. It doesn't matter if some players have one card fewer than the others.

Beginning with the player at dealer's left, each player must play a 7, or else add on to cards in suit-sequences ascending or descending from the 7s.

Once the ◆7 has been played, for example, the ◆8 and ◆6 can be played. If the ◆8 is played, you can play the ◆9, and so on. Sequences ascend to the king and descend to the ace. Once an end card is reached, fold up the row of cards and turn them over.

Whenever you have no card to play, pass and toss one chip into the "kitty." Whoever is out of cards first collects the chips in the kitty, plus one chip per card left in each player's hand.

Tips: Try to encourage play in suits where you have aces or kings. Your goal is to be able to hold back "stoppers": the 5s, 6s, 8s, and 9s that block everyone else's cards but not your own. If your timing is right, the suits you need help in will open up before your stoppers are gone.

GIN RUMMY

First introduced in 1899, Gin Rummy has become the most popular two-handed card game of all time. After Hollywood discovered it in the 1930s, Gin Rummy clubs started springing up all over the United States.

Number of Players: Two

Object: To match the cards you hold into melds of three cards or more. (See the rules for Rummy, page 142, for types of melds.)

The cards: A regular pack of 52 cards is used. Aces are low.

To play: Deal ten cards to each player, one at a time. Turn the next card face up to begin a discard pile; then place the rest of the pack face down beside this upcard to form the stock.

Nondealer begins play by taking this upcard (and then discarding) or by declining it. If nondealer declines it, dealer may take the upcard or also decline it. If both decline, nondealer takes the top card from the stock and then discards any card.

Once play starts, the two players continue alternately, taking the top discard or drawing a card from the stock, and then discarding.

Knocking: A player "knocks" by discarding face down and claiming "Knock." The player then lays down the hand in melds, with the "deadwood" (unmatched cards) separate. You can knock only if the total of your deadwood is less than 10 (see "Scoring"). Opponent then can lay off any deadwood on your melds. Melding all ten cards in your hand is called Gin; opponent then can't lay off deadwood on your melds.

The winner of one hand deals the next. When the stock is down to its final two cards, play ceases and the deal is thrown in.

Scoring: Cards count their face value, with face cards worth 10 points each. For Gin, score 25 points plus the value of all unmatched cards in your opponent's hand. For knocking, score the point value of your deadwood subtracted from opponent's deadwood after laying off.

Undercut (or underknock): Whenever opponent's remaining deadwood is less than or equal to knocker's, then opponent scores a 25-point bonus for the undercut, plus the point difference, if any.

The first player to reach 100 points wins the game.

Tips: Remember which cards have already been played. (Unless you decide otherwise, no player is allowed to look through the discards.) Especially remember the cards your opponent has picked up.

Your opponent will be watching the cards you pick up. Even when you're desperate to make matches, don't pick up a discard unless it melds for you—or at least gives you great chances.

It might pay to keep a card drawn from stock that just increases your melding chances or lowers your count, if by keeping it you can discard a high card.

The first player "knocks" with 4, the value of the unmatched ♦4. The second player melds ♣3-4-5-6 and the three 8s. The second player also lays off deadwood by adding the ♥Q-K to the ♥9-10-J run.

Try to keep cards that you can turn easily into melds. For example, ♦8-♦9-♠9 can use any of four cards to make a meld, whereas ♦9-♦J-♦K can be improved with only two cards, ♦10 or ♦Q.

High cards are usually safest to discard early in the play. Late in the game, even a high-card pair—like two queens—is a doubtful asset. They may become "isolated" from the rest of your cards, and your opponent who finds a late queen in the stock pile may decide to keep it rather than discard it.

Take notice when your opponent discards low cards early. It may mean he or she already has a high-card meld—or is still speculating on one.

The best policy for knocking is to do it as soon as possible. Don't be timid. Holding off a few turns to play for a Gin hand will often let your opponent get rid of some deadwood—or even make a hand better than your own—while yours doesn't improve.

Variations: Traditionally, when an ace is turned for the upcard, players must play for Gin only. Also, if the upcard is a spade, scores for that deal double. By agreement beforehand, players may adopt either rule or both.

GO FISH

For many of us, Go Fish may have been our first card game, and for some of us, it may still be the one that we continue to play best!

———◆———

Number of players: Two to six.

Object: To win the most sets of four cards ("books") by asking other players for them.

The cards: A regular pack of 52 cards is used, but you might "shorten" the pack in order to have a quicker game by removing all cards of a few different ranks.

To play: When two people play, deal seven cards each; otherwise, deal five cards each. Leave the undealt cards face down as a draw pile. Starting with the player at dealer's left, each player asks another for cards of a specific rank. For example: "Kevin, do you have any 6s?" In order to ask, you yourself must already have at least one 6. Kevin has to give you all the 6s he holds, but the other players do not.

If this is your hand, you can ask for 6s, 3s, 8s, Ks, 9s, or aces.

Whenever your request for a card is filled, it remains your turn. Continue with your turn, asking any player for cards of a specific rank. When the player you ask can't oblige, you'll be told to "Go Fish." Pick up the top card of the draw pile. If it's the rank you called for, show the card at once, and your turn goes on. Otherwise, your turn ends.

Play proceeds to the left in this fashion. Whenever you have collected all four cards of one rank (a "book"), show the other players, then place the book next to you in a compact pile.

Scoring: When all the cards have been drawn and all the books collected, whoever has gathered the most books wins.

Tip: Pay attention to who seeks which cards, for you will inevitably draw a card someone was looking for earlier. You can capture those cards at your next turn if you can remember whom to ask!

Variations: Call for cards from all players at once: The game moves faster when everyone must give up the wanted cards. This also makes it a better move to ask for a card when your book lacks just one, since whoever might have drawn the fourth one must give it to you.

An interesting scoring variant is to assign each book a value equal to its rank. Aces would then count 11, picture cards 10, and all other cards would be worth their pip (face) value.

HEARTS

In any of its numerous versions, Hearts is not difficult to play, but it's certainly not easy to master. An observant and calculating player will be a consistent winner. Actually, Hearts is a game for the loser in us, for if you hold a lot of low cards, you'll win!

———◆✦◆———

Number of players: Four is best, but two, three, or six may also play. The more common four-player version is explained first.

Object: To win as few of the penalty cards as possible (all the hearts as well as the ♠Q), or else—if the hand is strong enough—to win them all.

The cards: A regular pack of 52 cards is used. Aces are high.

To play: Deal cards one at a time, until each player has 13.

The pass: An interesting feature of Hearts is the pass, where each player sends three cards to another player. A popular method is to pass the cards to the

Point-scoring cards in Hearts. Try not to take these cards, or else try to take them all!

left on the first deal, to the right on the second deal, and across on the third deal, with no pass at all on the fourth deal. The cycle then repeats. Players may not look at the cards passed to them until they have completed their own pass.

Whoever holds the ♣2 now leads it. Follow suit if possible but if you can't, play any card other than a heart or the ♠Q. Whoever plays the highest card of the suit led wins the trick and leads to the next. For example, whoever plays the highest club on the first trick takes the cards played to that trick, and leads to the next.

Breaking hearts: You can't lead a heart until hearts have been "broken"—that is, until someone has discarded a heart already. However, if it's your lead and all you have are hearts, you must lead one.

Scoring: After all the tricks have been played out, count up the penalty cards you've taken. Count 1 for each heart, and 13 for the ♠Q. For instance, if your tricks include the ♠Q and the ♥6, ♥7, ♥9, ♥10, and ♥K, you would receive 18 points. The other three players would somehow score the remaining 8 points. Keep a running tally. The game ends when someone reaches 100 points or any other agreed-upon total. Whoever has the lowest score at the end is the winner.

Shooting the moon: If the tricks you win contain all the hearts and the ♠Q, this is called "shooting the moon." Subtract 26 points from your score if you accomplish this. (If you choose, you may add 26 points to everyone else's score. This would end the game more quickly.)

Tips: You generally want to avoid taking tricks; however, on most hands, you'll take a few. Your main concern is always to avoid the trick that includes the ♠Q. This affects the pass especially. If you are dealt the ♠Q, you may be safer keeping it if you have at least five spades. Otherwise it may be a danger in your hand and you should pass it, for the other players will lead spades. The ♠A and ♠K are risky to keep when you are "short" in spades, since they may be forced to capture the dreaded ♠Q. Spades lower than the ♠Q are usually very safe to keep, since none can capture the ♠Q!

Sometimes it's best to pass all your cards in a "short" suit with no low cards, since you'd be forced to win tricks in that suit otherwise. On some hands it may be wise to pass cards in a variety of suits to increase the likelihood of everyone following suit.

If you are thinking of shooting the moon, pass away all hearts that might be losers, since suspicious

Your hand before a right-hand pass. You should pass the ♠Q, ♦9, and ♥6. With the ♠Q on your right, the ♠A is not a dangerous card! If you were passing left, you'd pass the ♠A instead of the ♥6.

players will not let you win any hearts of mid-rank if they suspect you're shooting.

Variations: There's practically an infinite number of ways that Hearts can be played, so make sure everyone is playing by the same rules. One popular rule is that the ♠Q must be discarded at its first available opportunity. This avoids accusations of a player holding it to "dump" on a specific opponent. Another widespread rule is to count either the ◆J or ◆10 as -10 points in favor of whoever wins it.

In some games, the pass is always to the left, while some prefer no pass at all; in others, the ♣2 isn't required to be led—instead, the player at dealer's left may lead any card at all.

For three players, discard the ◆2, leaving 51 cards, and deal 17 cards to each player. Pass four cards, not three. With more or fewer than four players, you can pass left and right, but not across.

Hearts for Two: This streamlined version for two players of the popular four-handed game retains a lot of the sport of the original version.

Object: To get the lower score. Hearts taken in tricks count 1 each, and the ♠Q taken in a trick counts 6. Or you can "shoot the moon," which means to take all of the hearts plus the ♠Q and score 19 for the other player.

The cards: A regular pack of 52 cards is used. Aces are high.

To play: Deal 13 cards to each player, one at a time. Put the remainder of the pack face down as the stock. Unlike the four-handed game, Hearts for Two does not permit exchanging cards before play. Non-dealer leads to the first trick.

You must follow suit if you are able to; otherwise, play any card. No suit is trump. The trick is taken by the higher card of the suit that is led. After each trick, both players take a new card from the stock, the winner of the trick drawing first.

The traditional adage of four-handed Hearts applies: Hearts may not be led until a heart has been discarded. Of course, should you have nothing but hearts, you must play one.

Although in four-handed Hearts the rule is to discard the ♠Q at the first opportunity, the two-handed version doesn't require it. The reason for the rule when more people are playing is to forestall charges of favoritism; this complaint can't arise in a two-handed game. However, if a player leads the ♠A, opponent must follow with the queen if able to. If a player leads ♠K, opponent also must follow with the queen or else win the trick with the ace.

Play continues until all tricks have been played out, even after the stock has been exhausted.

Scoring: Players count the hearts in the tricks they have taken and score a point for each. The player who took the ♠Q in a trick scores 6 points. Low score wins after ten hands. A successful moon shot scores 19 points for the other player.

Tips: You usually want to avoid taking tricks. When you win a trick, use a high card. When you lose a trick, also use a high card—for example, play the ♣10 under the ♣J.

Deuces are especially valuable, for they let you lose the lead as long as opponent can follow suit. Of course, once the deuce is played, the 3 becomes low in that suit.

If you void yourself in a suit, you can discard the ♠Q when that suit is led. As long as you have the queen, hold other spades as protection against opponent's spade leads.

If you do not have the ♠Q, and suspect that opponent may, lead spades lower than the queen.

To shoot the moon, a player will need enough high hearts to win every heart trick. Don't let opponent's hearts become too strong by discarding the wrong heart. From ♥A-10-2, discard the ♥10 and save the ♥A as insurance against a moon shot from opponent. You always have to sacrifice and win at least a heart or two to stop a moon shoot.

Variations: You may: count the ♦10 (some prefer the ♦J) as -5; require that clubs be led at the first trick; allow hearts to be led at any time; require the ♠Q to be played at the first opportunity; consider that playing the ♠Q does "break hearts"; count the ♠Q as 13 and the ♦J or ♦10 as -10, which are their traditional values in the four-handed game.

I DOUBT IT

I Doubt It is a hilarious game that is fun for children as well as adults. If you're the sneaky sort and have a suspicious mind, then this game is for you!

———◆═◆═◆———

Number of players: Two or more, but it's a greater challenge with at least three players.

Object: To be the first player to get rid of all your cards.

The cards: A regular pack of 52 cards is used for two to five players. Two packs of 52 cards are used for six or more players.

To play: Deal all the cards out, as evenly as possible. To save time, deal in twos or threes.

In turn, players discard one or more cards, announcing them by rank. Start with aces.

The player at dealer's left begins by saying, for example, "Two aces," placing two cards face down in the center of the table to begin a discard stack.

The following player announces "Deuces"—or perhaps "One deuce"—and puts a single card face down on the stack. The next player announces "3s" and so on, each player stating a rank just above the previous one played. After you reach kings, start play again at aces.

At your turn you must discard, but the cards you discard don't have to be the rank called for. You might announce "Three queens" and put two jacks and a 6, or any three cards. Be convincing. Anyone who is skeptical can challenge you by being first to shout "I doubt it!"

The challenge: If challenged, turn over your discards. If they're not what you claimed, pick up the

Lay successive discard packets crosswise, to avoid disputes. Here, a player has announced four 7s but has been caught playing two 6s, a 3, and an 8!

entire discard pack. But if your cards are as announced, your challenger picks up the stack!

Note that when you use a single pack, you can discard up to four cards. With a double deck, the discard can go as high as eight cards.

Tips: Often you'll need to make a phony discard. This may be easier to do when the discard stack is low. You may get away with a one-card lie.

As the pile grows, so do the risks of discarding and challenging. Also, you're sure to be challenged on your final discard. So, plan ahead to have at least one card of the rank you'll need.

It can be helpful to expand your hand by losing an occasional challenge.

Variation: In some games, there may be too many challenges, and you may want to bring order to them. One way to do this is to permit only the next player to say "I doubt it."

KALUKI

Spell it Kalooki, Caloochi, or Kalogghi, but this double-deck rummy game has been a longtime club favorite in America and Great Britain.

◆━◆×◆━◆

Number of players: Two to six.

Object: To be the first player to get rid of all the cards in your hand by creating melds.

The cards: Two regular packs of 52 cards plus their four jokers are used. Aces are high or low, but not both.

To play: With two to four players, deal 15 cards each. With five players, deal 13 to each, and with six, deal 11 each. Then turn one card up to start the discard pile. The remaining cards form the stock. A player cannot take the upcard until he has made an initial meld or can use the upcard immediately in a meld. Your first meld must total at least 51 points, which can include cards you lay off on other players' melds, keeping in mind that you have to table at least one meld of your own.

Value of cards in melding:

Ace	15 points
Face card	10 points
Plain card	pip value
Joker	value of the card it stands for

Melds are three or more cards of the same rank (no repeated suits), or three or more cards of the same suit in sequence. Aces can be high or low, but not both. For example, ◆Q-◆K-◆A and ◆A-◆2-◆3 are valid melds, but ◆K-◆A-◆2 is not.

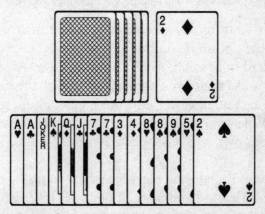

Pick up the ◆2 for a sequence (9 points), and use the joker as an ace, counting 15 (45 points). Since 9 + 45 = 54 points, you are able to meld. This doesn't even take into account any layoffs you may be able to make.

At your turn of play, you may swap a card for a joker that's melded as that card. In this meld, if you have the ◆9, exchange it for the joker, which you can use later however you choose.

Before your initial meld, when it is your turn, either take the upcard if you can meld it, or else take the top card from stock, meld if able, and discard. After your initial meld, you are entitled to pick the card showing and discard from your hand without melding. Whenever you meld, you may also lay off cards on your own and other players' melds.

Scoring: Each losing player pays the winner 1 point per card left in hand, and 2 points per joker left in hand. A player who goes out on a single play goes "Kaluki" and collects double from every player.

Tips: Usually it doesn't take many rounds for someone to go out, so there's no real advantage to delaying your initial meld.

Jokers are valuable. While they can be melded as a group for 15 points each, they are put to much better use individually.

Variations: In scoring, an alternate practice is to penalize players for the face value of the cards in their hand, with jokers counting 25 points each.

One version of Kaluki counts aces as 11, not 15, so agree among the players about this beforehand.

KLABERJASS

Try pronouncing this game "Klobber-yahss"—or just call it Klob. Probably Hungarian in origin, it became a favorite for gamblers in the United States as a one-on-one test of talent. Though Klaberjass is like Euchre in putting the jack atop the trump ladder, it is closer to the Bézique family. The game may seem complicated at first, but you'll pick it up after a few hands.

———◆◈◆———

Number of players: Two.

Object: To score points by declaring sequences and by winning high-counting cards in tricks.

Trump

Nontrump

The cards: A 32-card deck, A-K-Q-J-10-9-8-7 for each suit. The rank of trump cards is different from that in the other suits. Card rank in trumps: J (high), 9, A, 10, K, Q, 8, 7. Card rank in the other suits: A, 10, K, Q, J, 9, 8, 7.

To play: Deal six cards to each player, one at a time, and turn over an upcard to propose trump. Save the rest of the cards for further dealing.

Nondealer speaks first, saying "Pass," "Take," or "Schmeiss" (pronounced "shmice"). "Take" means nondealer accepts the suit turned up as trump, becoming the "maker," or player responsible for making the higher score. "Schmeiss" is an offer to throw the hand in. If dealer accepts, the cards are thrown in for a new deal. If dealer refuses, the schmeisser must become the maker with the upcard suit as trump. If nondealer passes, dealer then must pass, take, or schmeiss.

If you both pass on the first round, nondealer names a new trump suit or passes again. If the latter, dealer now names a new trump suit or passes. If both pass twice, the hand is thrown in, with no redeal; the deal alternates in Klaberjass.

Once a suit has been settled on for trumps, each player is then dealt another three cards, bringing the hands to nine cards. At this time it's also customary to turn up the bottom card of the deck.

If the original upcard was accepted as trump, either player with the 7 of trump may now exchange it for the upcard.

Sequences: Before playing out the tricks, determine which player, if either, has the highest sequence. Only the player with the highest-ranking sequence may score for sequences. For sequences only, each suit follows the order A-K-Q-J-10-9-8-7. Three or more cards in a row, all of the same suit, form a sequence.

A three-card sequence is worth 20 points; a four-card or longer sequence is worth 50 points. A 50-point sequence is higher than a 20-point sequence.

Between sequences of equal value, the one with the higher top card is higher. If the sequences tie in rank, a sequence in trump beats one not in trump. If neither is trump, nondealer's beats dealer's.

Nonmaker begins the dialogue, claiming "20" or "50" or "no sequence." Maker now answers, either declaring "no sequence," or agreeing that nonmaker's meld is "good"—or, if the sequences have equal value, by asking, "How high?"

As nondealer, with this hand, you could take hearts and probably win, but clubs would also be good as trumps. Pass now, giving opponent a chance to take or schmeiss. If opponent passes, you can name clubs on the second round.

The player whose sequence is high may also declare any other sequence, regardless of its value or rank. To score your sequences, you must show them before playing to the second trick. The other player scores no sequences.

Once the sequences dialogue is over, play begins. No matter who the maker is, nondealer always makes the first lead. Thereafter, the winner of a trick leads to the next one.

A trick is won by the higher trump in it or, if it has no trump, by the higher card. You must follow suit if able. If unable to follow suit, you must trump if possible; otherwise, you may discard. If a trump is led, you must play a higher trump if able.

Scoring: Each player earns points by taking certain cards in tricks.

Jack of trump ("Jass," pronounced "yahss")	20
9 of trump ("Menel," pronounced "muh-NIL")	14
Each ace	11
Each 10	10
Each king	4
Each queen	3
Each jack (not trump)	2
Last trick	10

Bella: If you hold the K-Q of trump, declare 20 points for "Bella" when you play the second of them to a trick.

Players combine this score with any melds or Bella. If maker's total is more than defender's, then both record their points. If maker and defender tie, defender's score only is recorded. If defender scores more than maker, credit defender with both scores. First player to 500 points wins.

Tips: You won't always have a rock-crusher of a hand in the first six cards. The last three cards received can be high trumps and nice cards for sequences, or useless losers, or a mix of the good and the bad. If you become the maker needing to fill in an open sequence, you probably won't get it. With two sequences open, your chances improve a good deal.

J-Q-K or J-9-A of trump is an obvious "take," but you may want to take with J-Q of trump plus some high tricks. Jack alone with two outside tricks is a very reasonable take. Also, to accept with A-K-Q of trump (40 points with Bella) and an outside ace will usually win—unless opponent has very high trumps or a 50 sequence.

The schmeiss is a unique feature of Klaberjass. As nondealer, schmeiss when you have only a fair chance to win with the trump proposed and fear opponent may make a big score picking a different suit for trumps. Otherwise, pass and name a good suit later.

When nondealer passes, dealer should accept or schmeiss if possible rather than allowing opponent to name a new trump suit.

If opponent is nearing 500 and you are rather behind, don't become maker unless you have a chance to win big. Otherwise opponent will score enough points simply as defender.

Variations: Some players allow nondealer a schmeiss on the second round, after two passes. For instance, "Schmeiss clubs" leaves dealer the choice to either throw the hand in or be the defender with clubs as trump. Dealer cannot schmeiss on the second round.

MICHIGAN

The many names of this game—Chicago, Saratoga, Newmarket, Stops, Boodle, and others—show its far-reaching appeal. Though played with cards and chips, it doesn't involve betting.

❖◆❖

Number of players: Two or more.

Object: To win chips by being the first player out of cards, and also by playing "money" or "boodle" cards.

The cards: A regular pack of 52 cards is used, plus an extra ♥A, ♣K, ♠Q, and ♦J (the "boodle" cards). Aces are high.

To play: Distribute an equal number of chips to each player. Place the four boodle cards face up in the center of the table, where they remain through-out play. Each player puts one chip on each boodle card.

Deal all the cards out, one at a time, dealing one hand more than players. For example, if there are four players, deal five hands. The extra hand, called

The layout of boodle cards.

the "widow," is dealt to dealer's left. It's all right if some players have one more card than others.

As dealer, look at your cards and decide if you wish to exchange them for the widow (without seeing it first). If you prefer, keep your original hand and auction the widow, still unseen, to the other players. The auction begins at one chip. Collect the chips bid for it, and keep them in your own hand. The high bidder wins the widow hand and must play it, but this player retains an advantage in knowing which cards will be out of play.

The player at dealer's left leads the lowest card held of any suit. Whoever has the next card in sequence in that suit plays it, and so on, until no one can play. For example, the ♥4 is led, the same player also plays the ♥5, and then other players follow with the ♥6, ♥7, and ♥8. No one has the ♥9, a "stopper," so whoever played the ♥8 now continues play, leading the lowest card of a different suit.

When an ace is played, the sequence ends. As always, begin a new sequence with your lowest card in another suit. Whenever you play a boodle card, collect the chips on it. If you play your last card, the deal ends and you win; collect the chips in the kitty

This hand has no boodle cards, no aces, and no other high cards to finish off the run of a suit. If this is your hand as dealer, swap it for the widow. If you're not the dealer, you should bid for the widow and get rid of this hand.

and also one chip from each player for every card you catch them with. The deal also ends when no one can play.

Leave all uncollected chips on the boodle cards. The deal passes to the left, and all players put another chip on each boodle card. Since the dealer has an

Here's the widow hand for which you traded the hand on page 95. This is a much better hand! Let's say the game is started with the ♣*7. You'll end the sequence with the* ♣*A, winning the* ♣*K boodle, and now, because you know which cards are out of the game, you can control the rest of play. Lead the* ♥*2. Since the* ♥*3 is a stopper, you go to a different suit, playing* ♠*4. The* ♠*5 is in the discards too, so you switch back to* ♥*6. This will play to your* ♥*9, again making a stop. Now the* ♠*J will play to your* ♠*A, and when you play the* ♦*8, the hand's over!*

advantage, the game ends after an agreed number of complete dealing rounds. Whoever has the most chips is the winner.

Tip: If you take the widow, remember the cards you threw away. This can help a lot in the play.

Variations: As an alternative to bidding for a widow hand, some prefer to set aside several or more stop cards that no one sees.

Some play that you pay an extra penalty if you're caught at the end holding a boodle card.

Another variant adds a fifth boodle, usually the sequence ♥9-♥10-♥J. Add cards to the layout from another deck, and anyone playing two of these cards in a row collects their boodle chips.

You can always use an A-K-Q-J of different suits for boodle cards, but if you use the 9-10-J sequence boodle, it should be the same suit as the ace.

NAP OR NAPOLEON

The emperor Napoleon Bonaparte was neither the inventor nor the popularizer of this game, but his name is used for one of the bids in the game. Two of his enemies, Wellington and Blucher, are also bids.

———◆◆◆———

Number of players: Two.

Object: To outbid the other player and then to win the number of tricks you've bid for.

The cards: A regular pack of 52 cards is used. Aces are high.

To play: Dealer deals five cards each in groups of three and then two. Starting with nondealer, each player must make one bid, naming a number of tricks to be won. The bid does not name desired trump suit, only number of tricks.

Bids in Nap:

1	1 trick
2	2 tricks
3	3 tricks
Misère (me-ZARE)	3 tricks, no trump suit
4	4 tricks
Napoleon	5 tricks
Wellington	5 tricks
Blucher	5 tricks

A Misère bid outranks a bid of 3. Napoleon, Wellington, and Blucher are all bids to take all five tricks, but each scores differently. This means that a player who bids Napoleon for five tricks can be outbid by the other player bidding Wellington or Blucher.

Either dealer or nondealer could bid 3.

Nondealer must bid 2 or pass. Dealer becomes the "maker" by bidding higher. If neither player bids, throw the hand in.

Maker begins by leading a card to the first trick. This card's suit becomes trump, except, of course, if the bid is Misère, which is no trump. You must follow suit when you are able to; otherwise you may trump or discard. A trick is won by the higher trump in it or, if it contains no trump, by the higher card. The winner of each trick leads to the next.

Scoring: If as maker you win the number of tricks you bid, score the number of points you bid. Nothing extra is scored for overtricks. If you bid and make Napoleon, Wellington, or Blucher, score 10 points.

A good Misère hand.

The opponent scores for defeating maker's bid. If maker doesn't take the number of tricks bid, opponent scores that number. Opponent scores 5 for defeating Napoleon, 10 for defeating Wellington, and 20 for defeating Blucher. It's the risk of greater loss that separates the three different bids for all five tricks.

Nap is a fast game to play. The first to reach 30 points—or a higher number if you like—is the winner.

Tips: Since only ten cards are in play at a time, the odds are better than eight to one against your opponent having any one particular card. Thus if you have K-Q of trump, that will win two tricks eight out of nine times on the average.

A-K-Q of trump are three easy tricks, but A-3-2 of trump will also take three tricks whenever opponent has zero or one card of the suit. Remember, you must lead a trump at the first trick, and in this case you'd lead the ace.

Bid Misère when you have three sure or probable tricks such as three aces, two aces and a king, or an ace and two kings. Also, as nondealer, bid Misère when you don't want a bid of 3 to be outbid by dealer bidding Misère. As nondealer with A-K-Q in

A reasonable hand for Nap.

one suit, Misère is the correct bid, since the
maker—the high bidder—leads first.

As nondealer, when you have a near-certain five easy
tricks, bid Blucher rather than Napoleon, to prevent
dealer from outbidding you. A Napoleon bid for
nondealer would be a hand with five probable winners, or even four sure winners in trump and just
about any other card. To defeat you, opponent
would need five trumps—or would have to hold
onto the right card to capture your last card.

OH HELL!

In Oh Hell!, it's not how good your cards are, but how good your luck and judgment are. The game does have its momentary upsets, so if you need a name that's a bit more tame, just call it "Oh Well!"

———◆◆◆———

Number of players: Three to seven; however, it is best with four or five players. One player should be scorekeeper.

Object: To make precisely the number of tricks you bid—no more, and no less.

The cards: A regular pack of 52 cards is used. Aces are high.

To play: A game of Oh Hell! consists of a series of rounds. On the first, deal each player one card; on the second, deal two cards; and on the third, deal three, increasing the deal by one card each hand until the top limit. For example, when four people play, deal 13 cards on the last round. With five players, deal ten cards on the last round. The deal goes to the left for each new round.

After dealing, turn up one card to designate trumps. If you turn over an ace or a deuce, however, play at "no-trump," with no suit as trumps. Also, whenever you deal all 52 cards, play at no-trump.

In a five-handed game, you hold this hand. Bid "One." You'll take the ace of trumps—it's a sure winner. If you're careful, you won't take another trick! Spades probably won't be led three times, and even so, the ♠10 shouldn't be a problem. The ♥5 is not likely to win, and the key will be to save the ♦3, a low trump, for a trick containing higher trumps. An ideal scenario would be for a club to be led, so you could trump it with the ♦A and then lead the ♦3.

The bidding: Starting at dealer's left, players state in turn the number of tricks they hope to win. The scorekeeper records each bid. The total number of tricks bid for on each deal must differ from the number of tricks available. Therefore, the scorer must require the last bidder—the dealer—to register a legal bid.

Once all the bids are recorded, the player at dealer's left leads any card desired. Always follow suit if possible, but play any card otherwise. Each trick is taken by the highest card in it of the suit led, or by the highest trump if it contains any trump. The winner of each trick leads to the following trick.

Scoring: After all the tricks have been taken, the scorekeeper tallies how everyone fared. If you made your bid exactly, score 1 point per trick plus a 10-point bonus. (With the example hand, you'd score 11.) If you failed, however, subtract 10 points for each trick you're off, whether it's more or less than your bid. The player with the most points after the last deal wins. It's not unusual to end up with a negative score, by the way.

Tips: Bidding in the first few rounds can be tricky, since so few cards from the pack are in play, and some bids are forced. In the early deals, you'll be surprised to see your low cards win tricks, while your aces get trumped. In most deals, you can count on low cards to be losers more reliably than counting on high cards to be winners (unless they're high trumps).

When the bid-total is above the number of tricks in the deal, other players will be quite willing to capture your questionable middle-range cards or trump a trick that you have the high card on. However, when the bid-total is under the trick-total, players will be happy to let you win an extra trick or two.

Variations: Some players prefer to write down bids secretly. In this case, it's okay for the bid-total and the trick-total to turn out equal. Those bids can be revealed either before the first lead or after the last trick.

In many games, once the highest possible number of cards have been dealt, the game continues with the number of cards per hand decreasing by one each hand, until a final one-card deal.

OLD MAID

Many of us think Old Maid requires a special pack of cards, but actually its ancestral form some 150 years ago likely used a regular pack minus one card.

———◆◆◆———

Number of players: Three or more is best, though two can play.

Object: Not to be left holding the "Old Maid."

The cards: A pack of 51 cards is used, made by removing one queen from a regular pack.

To play: Deal all the cards out one at a time. Before play starts, each player shows and retires any pairs of like rank. After that, the player at dealer's left takes one card, unseen, from the player at his left. If this makes a pair, it is also tabled, and the player continues. When the card taken does not make a pair, play passes on to the next player, who in turn takes a card from the next player. In this way all cards eventually pair up except one queen, and the player holding it is declared "Old Maid."

When drawing cards from your neighbor's hand, make sure that only the card backs can be seen.

Tip: After one pair of queens has been tabled, only body language can tell you who might have the remaining lone queen. Even so, it's hard to know which card that queen might be. Is the player in the diagram encouraging you to take the card sticking out? Is that card safe? Unless you know, it's simply a matter of luck to avoid the Old Maid.

Variations: Instead of removing a queen, randomly remove from the pack one card which no one sees. In this way, only at the very end will all the players discover which card in actuality was the "Old Maid."

For a quicker game, you can shrink the pack by omitting all cards of several ranks.

PANGUINGUE

Panguingue, or Pan, a gambling game especially popular out West, can also be enjoyed as a party game. It grew out of Coon Can and uses the same cards, only it uses more of them! It also has a language of its own.

———◆◆◆◆———

Number of players: Up to 15, though best when limited to eight.

Objects: To meld certain groups of cards ("conditions"), and to be the first to "go out" (meld all cards).

The cards: Five or more Coon Can packs (regular packs of 52 cards with all 8s, 9s, and 10s omitted) are shuffled together. Aces are low.

To play: Unlike in other games, in Pan the deal and play rotate counterclockwise (to the right).

Deal ten cards to each player, in batches of five. Leave the remaining stock in the center of the table, turning its top card over to begin a discard pile.

Dropping: Each player decides whether to drop or play after looking at his hand. If you drop, throw in two chips. These chips will go to the winner of the hand. Dropping is also known as "going on top," because the forfeited cards are stacked on the foot of the stock. The discards don't belong to the stock and cannot be played.

If you decide to play, you must stay in until the end. The closest remaining player to dealer's right goes first. The object of play is to meld 11 cards. A meld must consist of at least three cards in a group or sequence. A sequence is any three cards of the same suit, in sequence; a group is three or more cards of the same rank.

SPECIAL TERMS IN PAN:

Condition. A spread that pays to its owner.

Going on top. Dropping out before play starts.

Non-comoquers. All kings and aces.

Rope. A sequential meld.

Spread. Any meld.

Square cards. As, 2s, 4s, 6s, Js, Qs, Ks.

Valle cards. 3s, 5s, 7s.

PAYOFF MELDS (CONDITIONS)

Same-suit valle melds

2 chips   4 chips

Valle melds in different suits

1 chip   1 chip

Same-suit square cards

1 chip   2 chips

Low or high sequence

1 chip   2 chips

At each turn, you may take the upcard if you can meld it or add it on to a meld you already have. Otherwise, draw the top card of the stock. After drawing, table any melds you may have, and discard one card.

There are two types of melds: payoff melds (conditions) and non-payoff melds. When you lay down a condition, each active player immediately pays you according to the chart below. Note that spades score double in all conditions.

All 3s, 5s, and 7s are "valle" cards, meaning they are cards that have value. Cards of any other rank ("square" cards) do not have value.

Any group of valle cards, different suits	1 chip
Any group of valle cards, same suit	2 chips (4 chips in spades)
Any group of non-valle cards, same suit	1 chip (2 chips in spades)
Any sequence of A-2-3	1 chip (2 chips in spades)
Any sequence of J-Q-K	1 chip (2 chips in spades)

NON-PAYOFF MELDS

Sequence of three or more

Non-comoquers
(kings and aces in groups of three or more, any suits)

Other square cards, must be three different suits

Groups of three or more square cards must be three different suits. With three different suits, however, you can lay off any duplicates at that time as well.

Sequences must be either low or high; for example, ♥K-♥A-♥2 is not a valid meld. ♣5-♦6-♠7 is not a valid meld either, because a sequence must be all of the same suit.

Laying off cards: You may lay off cards onto your own melds, but not onto other players' melds. Whenever you lay off an additional card on a pay spread, you are paid again by each player. Exception: Payment for extending a same-suit valle card spread pays half—just 1 chip, and 2 in spades.

By taking the ♥6 (the fourth card from the meld) and adding it to the ♥5 and ♥7 from your hand, you form a "rope."

Here, the cards have been rearranged to form a condition in spades! Collect 2 chips from every player.

Switching: You can rearrange or switch your own melds in two ways: You can take the fourth of a group and use it in another meld, and you can re-shape sequence melds.

Forcing: If at your turn the top discard can be laid off onto your melds, you are not obliged to take it unless another player demands that you do. This is called forcing. Upon adding the card to your meld, you must then discard.

Scoring: Whoever goes out first is the winner. Winner receives 1 chip from every player who did not drop, plus additional payment for all his conditions. In effect, then, the winner is paid twice for his pay-off melds.

Tips: The most important decision is whether to play a hand or pay the penalty and "go on top." Usually you should stay in a hand if it contains valle cards and others that may give you pay spreads. You should also stay in the game if your cards work together and your hand offers good possibilities of melding.

Variations: Panguingue houses often use a special pack. From eight Coon Can packs, one suit of spades is omitted, leaving 310 cards. Sometimes an extra ♠3, ♠5, ♠7, ♠2, and ♠Q are also removed. In such games, the player with the lowest card receives the first deal, and thereafter the winner of each deal receives cards first.

PINOCHLE

Although Auction Pinochle is perhaps the most competitive form, two-handed Pinochle was probably the most popular card game for two in the United States before the advent of Gin Rummy.

————◆◆◆————

Number of players: Two.

Object: To score the most points by melding and by taking tricks.

The cards: A double deck—what's known as a Pinochle deck—each deck consisting of A, K, Q, J, 10, 9 of each suit (48 cards total). The cards rank A, 10, K, Q, J, 9.

To play: Deal 12 cards to each player; turn the next card up to designate the trump suit. If it's a 9, dealer scores an immediate 10 points. The remaining cards form a stock pile.

Every deal has two phases: trick-taking with melding and the endgame. To begin the first phase, non-dealer leads any card; dealer may follow by playing any card—you don't have to follow suit. Each trick is won by the higher trump, or if it contains no trump, by the higher card of the suit led. If the two cards are identical, the first one played wins.

Winner of the trick may meld any one of these:

Pinochle (♠Q-♦J)	40 points
♠A-♥A-♣A-♦A ("100 aces")	100 points
♠K-♥K-♣K-♦K ("80 kings")	80 points
♠Q-♥Q-♣Q-♦Q ("60 queens")	60 points
♠J-♥J-♣J-♦J ("40 jacks")	40 points
K and Q, same suit (marriage)	20 points
Marriage in trump	40 points
A-10-K-Q-J of trump (flush)	150 points
Each 9 of trump ("dix," pronounced "deece")	10 points

Though a player may hold more than one meld in hand, after winning a trick only one melding combination may be tabled. Another trick must be won to make the second meld. This does not apply to the 9s of trump. The first dix can be exchanged for the upcard to get a higher trump. The second is simply shown to opponent and the 10 points scored.

A melded card may be used again in a different meld. For example, the ♠Q may be melded with the ♠K in a marriage; then after winning a later trick, the same ♠Q may be melded with a ♦J in a pinochle, or with ♣Q-♥Q-♦Q for 60 queens. A second marriage in spades would require a new ♠Q and ♠K. Cards melded on the table still belong to the hand of their owner and may be played to any trick. However, cards taken in tricks are out of play for the rest of the hand.

After a trick is won and any meld tabled, both players take a new card from the stock, the winner of the trick drawing first. Winner of the trick then leads to the next trick.

A player cannot meld 40 jacks and later meld 60 queens, also claiming the 40 points for pinochle. The player should first meld the pinochle and later meld the jacks and queens.

Endgame play: When only the upcard and a single stock card are left, the winner of the trick takes the stock card, and the loser takes the upcard (which at this point will be the 9 of trump). No further melds may be made. Players return to their hands any cards melded on the table, and the winner of the last trick starts the endgame by leading any card.

In playing the tricks during the endgame, a player must follow suit if able; otherwise, the player must trump if able. When a trump is led, opponent must play a higher trump if able. The object is to take tricks with high-scoring cards.

Scoring: After all the tricks have been played, players total up cards won as follows:

Each ace	11 points
Each 10	10 points
Each king	4 points
Each queen	3 points
Each jack	2 points
Last trick	10 points

Scorekeeper adds these trick points to each player's melds and reports the running totals. Game is usually played to 1000 points. If both players go over 1000 points on the same deal, whoever has the higher total wins.

Tips: Cards played to tricks in the first phase of the game are no longer available for melding. Play a possible melding card only if you're sure you can spare it. Win tricks with 10s, not with aces (unless you have a duplicate of that ace).

Kings and queens (especially the ♠Q) are good melding cards. Retain these cards while the possibility of melding with them is still alive. Jacks are not valuable cards to keep for melding (except the ♦J). Four different jacks score only 40 points, so unless you have this meld, don't keep jacks.

If you've seen both ♦Ks, then all other kings become less valuable, since 80 kings is no longer a possible meld.

If your opponent plays a good melding card early, it's likely to be a duplicate. However, they may be missing the rest of the meld and be strapped for a play.

Use a trump in beginning play to meld some cards and free them for play, or to prevent opponent from melding. In the endgame a long trump suit will bring in several extra tricks, as well as the last trick.

In the endgame, beware the singleton ace. If opponent plays the other ace, you follow suit and lose. Play yours first.

PIQUET

Piquet is over 550 years old! Legend says it was invented by a knight who fought with Joan of Arc. In 1743, Piquet was one of five games covered in a treatise on games. Packed with French verbiage, Piquet has flourished in England.

Number of players: Two.

Object: To outscore your opponent over six deals (a "partie").

The cards: A pack of 32 cards is used. (Remove all 2s through 6s from a standard pack.) Aces are high.

To play: Deal 12 cards to each player and place the remaining eight cards in a face-down "talon." Non-dealer may then choose to discard at least one and not more than five cards in exchange for an equal number of cards from the top of the talon. If non-dealer exchanges fewer than five cards, he may peek at those he did not take. Dealer may then exchange for as many cards as nondealer has left behind. The goal of both players in this exchange is to form scoring combinations (see "Declaring").

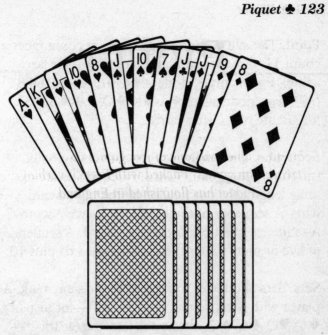

Nondealer discards ♠7, ♦9, and ♦8 and takes the top three talon cards. Since nondealer discarded only three cards, he may peek at the next two talon cards and put them back in place.

Carte blanche: When you're dealt no picture cards, you have "carte blanche." Before the exchange, show your hand to your opponent and score 10 points.

Declaring: After the card exchanges, the players determine who has the better scoring combinations in three categories: point, sequence, and sets, in that order.

Point. The suit with the highest point count (aces count 11, face cards 10, and pip cards their face value). For example, dealer's ♠A-♠Q-♠J-♠10-♠8 (49) beats nondealer's ♦A-♦K-♦Q-♦9-♦8 (48), for a score of 5 (1 per card).

Sequence. The longest sequence in a single suit (minimum three cards) wins. If sequences are of the same length, the one headed by the higher card wins. A sequence of three cards (a "tierce") scores 3. A sequence of four (a "quart") scores 4. A sequence of five or more scores the number of cards plus 10.

Sets. Sets of three or four cards of the same rank. A player with a foursome (a "quatorze")—for instance, ♦Q-♥Q-♣Q-♠Q—beats a threesome (a "trio")—♠A-♣A-♥A—regardless of rank; but in sets the same size, then the highest rank scores. Trios score 3 and quatorzes 14.

Nondealer begins the dialogue, starting with point. In the example given, nondealer would say "48" to which dealer would say, "Not good, 49." In each group, only the player with the winning meld scores. That player may also score for all other qualifying melds in that category. If players tie for best in a category, neither scores. For strategic reasons, you may choose not to declare a meld. This is called "sinking the meld."

Nondealer

Dealer

Dealer has a great-looking hand, but nondealer's is even better. (Nondealer's hand is the same one as illustrated on page 58 after the three exchange cards: ♥Q-♥9-♣9.) Nondealer's point is a seven-card suit (♥A-♥K-♥Q-♥J-♥10-♥9-♥8) with a higher count than dealer's (♣A-♣K-♣Q-♣10-♣9-♣8-♣7). Nondealer scores 7 for point. Nondealer's seven-card sequence is worth 17, and his three-card sequence (♠J-♠10-♠9) is worth 3: Nondealer scores 20 in sequences. Nondealer also has a group of four (♥J-♠J-♣J-♦J), which beats dealer's trios (aces, kings): Nondealer scores 14 for this quatorze. However, dealer, beaten in every category, does not score at all!

The play: Play to 12 tricks with no trump. Non-dealer leads any card to the first trick. The highest card of the suit led wins the trick, and the winner of a trick plays to the next. In the play, score 1 point for every trick you lead to, and 1 for every trick opponent leads that you win. For example, if non-dealer wins the first two tricks but loses the third, nondealer has still scored the first 3 points of play. The winner of the last trick scores 1 bonus point. Whoever wins more tricks scores a 10-point bonus, but if one player wins all 12 tricks, called a "capot," the bonus is 40 points. Thus, if you lead and win all 12 tricks, you score 53 (12 for the leads, 1 for last trick, and 40 for capot).

Scoring: If you score the first 30 (or more) points of a hand, you score either the "pique" or "repique" bonus.

Repique bonus (60 points): If either player scores 30 or more points just in card combinations before opponent scores any, he wins the 60-point repique bonus.

Pique bonus (30 points): If nondealer scores the first 30 points in card combinations and trick-taking, he earns a 30-point bonus for pique. Dealer cannot win pique, because nondealer automatically scores 1 for leading.

By custom, players announce their running totals throughout the hand, writing scores down at the end. Deal alternates, with six deals constituting a Piquet "partie," or game. At the end of the partie, if both players have more than 100 points, the winner gets the difference in scores, plus a 100-point game bonus. However, if the loser has under 100 points, the winner, regardless of score, gets both scores combined, as well as the 100-point game bonus. The loser is said to be rubiconned, having not crossed the "rubicon" of 100 points.

Tip: In play, much depends on who leads first. Take a look at the hand shown on page 125. Switch the players' seats and dealer would take every trick, if only dealer could go first! This rule affects your card-exchanging strategy. Dealer may need to keep strength in each suit to avoid giving up a capot. On the other hand, nondealer can discard all cards of a suit, to increase the chance of a capot.

Variation: Instead of playing a Piquet partie, play *Piquet au Cent,* in which the game ends as soon as one player reaches 100 points.

POKER

Poker has endless variants, but they fall into three main groups: Draw Poker, Stud Poker, and Hold 'Em Poker. The standard poker game rewards the best (highest) hand, but there are numerous forms of Lowball Poker where the worst hand wins. In recent years, there's been a surge of High-Low Poker, where the best hand and the worst hand get to divide the same pot. Many poker sessions are "dealer's choice," where the dealer picks from a bunch of games the players know.

Object: To win the pot, either by being the only player left or by having the best cards.

General Poker rules:
- Each player receives a stack or stacks of chips.
- Deal and betting proceed clockwise (to the left).
- At the showdown (end of the hand) the last to bet—or to raise the bet—shows first.
- Players calling the final bet have a right to see the cards of all others who call.
- If at any point only one player is left, that hand wins and need not be shown.

Rank of hands in Poker:
Royal flush: Five sequential cards of the same suit to the ace. (♥10-♥J-♥Q-♥K-♥A)
Straight flush: Any five sequential cards of the same suit. (♥7-♥8-♥9-♥10-♥J)
Four of a kind: All four cards of a rank. (♣6-♥6-♦6-♠6)
Full house: Three of a kind plus a pair. (♥3-♠3-♣3-♦10-♠10)
Flush: Any five cards of a suit. (♠Q-♠9-♠8-♠5-♠2)
Straight: Five cards in sequence, any suits. Ace can be either high or low. (♦A-♥2-♣3-♦4-♠5)
Three of a kind: Three cards of one rank, the rest unmatched. (♠K-♦K-♥K-♣9-♦7)
Two pair: Two different pairs of two cards of a rank, the rest unmatched. (♦J-♣J-♥8-♣8-♥5)
One pair: Two cards of a rank, the rest unmatched. (♦J-♣J-♥8-♣7-♥5)
High card: No combination. Aces are high. (♣A-♠7-♥9-♣10-♣4)

Between hands of the same type, the higher-ranked hand wins. For example, a flush headed by a jack (♣J-♣9-♣5-♣3-♣2) beats a flush to the 10 (♦10-♦9-♦8-♦5-♦3); queens up (♥Q-♦Q-♣3-♠3-♥4) beats 9s up (♠9-♥9-♣8-♥8-♠K).

Wild cards: In some games, dealer may call certain cards "wild"—that is, they can stand for any other card. Sometimes a joker is added as a wild card. Deuces wild (all four of them) is another popular choice. Another favorite is "One-eyes wild" (the three face cards in profile: ♦K, ♥J, and ♠J).

Lowball Poker: Lowball Poker can be played in as many styles as "high only" poker. There is usually a round of betting, a draw, then another betting round and a showdown. Aces rank low. The hand that ranks as the poorest poker hand wins. For example,

---

GENERAL TERMS IN POKER:

Ante. An initial stake each player puts in.

Betting in the blind. Betting without seeing your cards.

Bluffing. Betting or raising with a weak hand.

Broadway. A straight to the ace.

Call. To equal a bet made by another player.

Check. To pass.

Drop. To quit a hand.

Fold. To quit a hand.

(the) Goods. A real hand, no bluff.

Hole cards. In stud poker, face-down cards.

Openers. A good enough card combination to meet a minimum requirement.

♠7-♣3-♥9-♦4-♣5 (a 9-low) beats ♥4-♣A-♦2-♠J-♥3 (a jack-low).

Most lowball versions disregard flushes and straights and pay attention only to the number value of the cards, so that 7-6-5-4-3 is a 7-low. (Make very sure that all players are clear on this.) When hands competing for low have the same worst cards, look to the next worst card. For example, 8-5-4-2-A beats 8-6-3-2-A.

GENERAL TERMS IN POKER: *(CONTINUED)*

Pat hand. A hand you don't draw to.

Pot. All the bets in the center of the table.

Pot limit. A dangerous game, where the bet limit is the sum of chips in the pot.

Raise. To equal another's bet and add to it.

Sandbag. To check (pass), and later raise in the same round.

See a bet. To equal it, call.

Sixth street. The last upcard in seven-card stud, before a downcard is dealt.

Stand pat. Draw no cards.

Trips. Three of a kind.

Wheel. A hand good for both "high" and "low."

High-Low Poker: In High-Low Poker, the best hand and the worst hand divide the pot. Any form of poker—Draw, Stud, or Hold 'Em—can be played High-Low. High-Low differs from one-winner poker games in several important ways.

The declaration: In most games, players declare, before the showdown, whether they are going "high," "low," or "high and low." In some games, this is done out loud, by going around the table starting with the last raiser or bettor. This reduces some surprises and gives a certain positional advantage for which to play.

A more common practice is to declare silently, but at the same time. This can be done using chips or coins. At a signal, players either put no chips in their hand to go low, one chip in their hand to go high, or two chips to go high and low. In some games, this is the final action, after which the winners and losers are sorted out. In some games these declarations are followed by one more betting round (the "drive") that gives bluffers and legitimate hands one more chance to raise the pot. Since one player may have a lock on half the pot, High-Low poker limits raises to three per round.

Most High-Low games encourage you to go for high and low on the same deal, if you've got the right hand. This is easy in seven-card games, where you can use different sets of cards for each direction you go. In five-card games, it must be clear whether a 2-3-4-5-6 straight can be low, that is, a "6-low." If you go high-low but lose in either direction (high or low), you're out of the hand.

In any kind of poker, it's important that all players know the bet limits and the rules and agree to the games being played.

DRAW POKER

Number of players: Two to seven.

The cards: A regular pack of 52 cards is used.

To play: Each player antes one chip. Cards are dealt one by one until each player has five. The first player then may bet or check, but once a player has bet, each player in turn either folds or sees the bet (and perhaps raises it).

Once all bets and raises have been called, the dealer proceeds to ask each player in turn how many cards they wish to draw. The maximum number of cards a player can draw is three. Each player casts unwanted cards aside, and the dealer deals replacements. Dealer's own draw should be clearly announced, for example, the dealer may state, "Dealer takes two." A player who draws no cards is said to "stand pat."

Once players have all received their new cards, the final round of betting takes place, beginning with the player who made the last raise or bet. Most games establish a betting limit, which on the second round is usually double the first.

When all bets and raises have again been called, there is a showdown to see whose hand is best. Usually the last bettor shows first, and others may choose to fold their hands if beaten. However, the remaining players in the pot have a right to see all hands that have called.

If all players pass on the first round, throw the hand in. The deal passes to the left, and another round of five cards is dealt. Leave the chips in the pot, as players add another ante.

Tips: Most fairly serious poker games should have house rules that all players know in advance of play. For example, many games limit the number of raises in a round to three, unless only two players remain, who can then raise and re-raise each other as they wish. Other matters to clarify ahead of time include misdeals, misstatements of hands, maximum bets, and buying new chips, among others.

Variation: In *Jacks or Better,* the player who makes the first bet (the "opener") must have a pair of jacks or higher. These openers must be shown if asked later in the hand. If no one has an opener, each player re-antes for a new deal. In this way, the pot grows if no one can open. Some play that "progressive" openers are needed on each next hand: queens, then kings, then aces, then two pair, then back to aces, and so on.

HOLD 'EM POKER

Number of players: Two to ten.

Object: To join your two cards with any three on the table to make the best hand.

The cards: A regular pack of 52 cards is used.

To play: After each player antes, deal two cards face down to each player and five cards face down in the center of the table. Starting with the player at dealer's left, each player may check or bet. Once a player has made a bet, subsequent players must fold unless they see—or raise—the bet.

Once all first-round bets are called, the dealer turns over the first three face-down cards. These are called the "flop." You must use both your hole cards with three from the table in order to form the best possible hand.

Whoever was the last bettor starts a new round of betting, after which the dealer turns up one more card from the center of the table. Another betting round ensues, and then the dealer turns over the last card for a final betting round. After all calls have been made, whoever has the best hand and is still in the betting wins the pot.

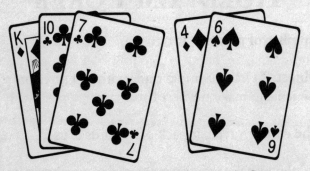

The three cards on the left make up the flop.

Tips: This is a game with no surefire advice, for each hand is different, and many different factors affect what the other players do. Some combinations, such as ♣K-♣Q, may seem to have greater prospects than ♦2-♠7, but if the flop is ♥7-♥2-♦7, you'd rather have the second hand. By betting on the first round with ♣K-♣Q, however, the ♦2-♠7 might drop before the flop.

Variations: Many varieties of Hold 'Em exist, and new ones are constantly being invented. One popular alternative is to deal players three cards rather than two. In this version, players choose two cards of the three from their hands to use, along with any three on the table. This makes the average winning hand a better one.

A popular practice is to require the first hand to toss in a bet "in the blind" (without seeing their cards), and the second hand then to follow with a "raise in the blind." The next players may choose to either drop, call, or raise. This invites players to call with moderate cards.

STUD POKER

Number of players: Two to eight.

The cards: A regular pack of 52 cards is used.

To play: In five-card stud poker, each player antes. Deal one card down and one up to each player, as shown below.

The player with the highest card showing starts by checking or by betting. As soon as there's a bet, the players following must, in turn, either fold or call—and perhaps raise—the bet.

Once all bets are called, the remaining players each receive another upcard. Another round of betting follows, started by the player with the best hand showing.

Each round of cards dealt up is followed by a betting round. The final round of bets occurs when all players left in the hand have four upcards. This round of betting should have a higher limit than the previous rounds. Also, if any player shows a pair at any time, the bet limit is raised.

After the final bets, the bettor—or last raiser—is usually first to turn over the hole card. If no one

Dealer

The ♣K is the high card. This player may check or bet. If ♣K bets, then the player with the ♥10 sees the bet, or else drops (shown by turning the ♥10 over), and so on with each player around the table. Since the ♣K was dealt first, it has betting priority over the ♥K.

You and one player remain from the hand dealt on page 139. You now show a pair of kings. Your opponent must have an ace in the hole to have any chance to win. If you have a king, 6, or 4 in the hole, you are a sure winner. Bet only as much as you think your opponent might call. If you are not a sure winner, however, you must decide what to do. In situations like this, a "poker face" is called for!

calls the last bet or raise, the winner gathers the pot and isn't obliged to show anyone the winning hand.

Variations: In seven-card stud poker, the mechanics work just as in five-card stud, except that two hole cards are dealt before the first upcard. After a fourth upcard is dealt to each player, the next card is again dealt down, in the hole. After this, one more betting round ensues.

Anytime a pair is showing, a higher bet limit applies. After the sixth and seventh cards, the higher bet limit also applies. To decide the pot, players use their best five cards out of the seven cards dealt.

RUMMY

Rummy originated in the camps and saloons of the old West, where it was known as Whiskey Poker because it was played for drinks. As times changed, so did the game. It received many new names and traveled in many directions, leaving favorite versions all around. Every Rummy game has its own appeal.

———◆◆◆———

Back in the 1930s, Gin was a minor branch of the Rummy family tree, just becoming known, when suddenly it was embraced by all the Hollywood stars. This link to the cinema's elite quickly turned Gin Rummy into a national craze. It remains one of the all-time-best two-handed games.

One of the interesting parts of Old-Fashioned Rummy—also known as Straight Rummy—is that although you cannot knock, you do have plenty of opportunities to lay cards off. 500 Rummy, a topsy-turvy type of Rummy, has also been called Pinochle Rum and Michigan Rum. In this version, everyone gets points for melds, and instead of trying to go out, you try to stay in and rack up a higher and higher score.

Melds in all Rummy games: Melds in Rummy consist of groups of three or more cards of the same rank or sequences of three or more cards in one suit.

Sample melds in Rummy.

GIN RUMMY

Number of players: Two or three, or four can play as partners.

Object: To meld your cards, and score for "Gin" or "Knock."

The cards: A regular pack of 52 cards is used. Aces are low.

To play: Deal ten cards to each player. Turn one card up—the "knock" card—to begin a discard pile, placing the remaining cards face down next to it as a draw pile.

Nondealer may take the knock card and discard. If nondealer declines the knock card, dealer may take it and discard. Should neither player want it, non-dealer draws the top card from stock and discards.

Turns alternate. At each play, take either the top discard or the top card from stock and then discard. Look to match cards in your hand into melds. When all your cards are melded, call "Gin" (or "Gin Rummy"), discard face down, and show your hand.

Knocking: If you wish to stop the round before you or your opponent reaches gin, you may knock. Simply discard face down and say "Knock." Or, simply rap the table. Put down your melds, setting aside your unmatched cards—called "deadwood." Your total deadwood count must not be greater than the original knock card (see "Scoring" for card values). If the knock card was ♦8 and you have ♣10-♣J-♣Q-♣K, ♠9-♣9-♥9, ♦A, ♠2, ♣4, your

MELDS IN GIN

Groups of three or four cards of the same rank.

Sequences of three or more consecutive cards in one suit. Aces are low only.

deadwood cards offer little melding hope. Since their count totals only 7, however, you should knock.

Laying off: After a player knocks, opponent has the opportunity to "lay off" any possible melds onto the tabled melds. In this way, opponent can reduce his point total (see "Scoring"). Laying off is not permitted after a Gin.

Scoring: Unmelded picture cards count 10, and all others their pip value (aces count 1). If you Gin, score your opponent's deadwood total, plus a 25-point bonus. If you knock, score the difference between your knock-count and opponent's remaining deadwood cards after making any layoffs.

As sometimes happens—especially after laying off—your knock count may be greater than your opponent's deadwood. In this case, opponent scores the difference in count, if any, plus a 20-point bonus for the underknock (also called "undercut"). If your opponent lays off every unmelded card, the bonus is 25 points for "ginning off."

Should neither player make Gin or knock, the hand is thrown in. Common practice is to stop play when two talon cards are still left. Game is generally played to 100 points.

Tips: Gin is a good game for memory-training: It will pay to recall which cards have already been played, especially the ones taken by your opponent. Be aware, however, that your opponent will also notice the discards you pick up!

A few helpful "don'ts":
• Don't pick up a discard unless it gives you a meld, or unless you have a very poor hand and your

pick opens up a few chances. An exception might be to pick up a low-count discard (an ace or deuce) when you have a bad hand and a safe discard to make.

- Don't hold on to a high melding chance that only one card can fill. For instance, don't hold on to ♦10-♦Q if you can draw any better or lower cards.
- Don't expect to find a third ace when you have two, unless you get lucky and draw it from the talon. That's not a card your opponent would discard except with a very good hand.
- Don't play for Gin when you can knock early.

Variations: When the upcard turned is an ace, it's a common practice to play the hand for Gin—knocking isn't allowed. Many people play that you count the hand double if the upcard is a spade. Another custom is for nondealer to receive an eleventh card, with no upcard turned. Play begins with nondealer's discard. You may knock any time your deadwood count is 10 or less.

In *Three-Handed Gin Rummy*, it's more difficult to reach a Gin hand, unless you allow both opponents a shot at the discard.

KNOCK RUMMY

Number of players: Two to five is best, but six may play.

Object: To knock when you have a lower deadwood count than any of your opponents.

The cards: A regular pack of 52 cards is used. Aces are low.

To play: For two players, deal ten cards each. For three or four players, deal seven cards each. With five or six players, deal just six cards each, leaving enough cards for each player to have several turns.

Knock Rummy proceeds like Gin Rummy, with two major differences. The first difference is that you may knock on any turn, with any deadwood count, and the second is that no cards are laid off on the knocker's melds.

As the play rotates, the discard is available only to the player whose turn it currently is.

Scoring: When someone knocks, show your cards, separating melded combinations from deadwood.

Whoever has the lowest deadwood count wins the difference from each other player. If you knock and are tied, the player you tie with is deemed the winner, and collects from the others. When you knock and do not have the lowest hand, pay an extra 10 points to the winner of the hand.

When you knock with a fully melded hand ("going rummy"), you win a 25-point bonus from each player, in addition to their deadwood counts.

Tips: With two players, if you're dealt a deadwood count in the 40s, that may often be lower than your opponent's count. Since losing costs an additional 10-point penalty, however, you should probably make a quick knock only if under 35.

With more players, the added bonus for "going rummy" may influence you to play out a hand with an early meld. That's okay if your deadwood cards are relatively high (7s and above) or if your unmelded cards have a good chance of making a meld. But if your deadwood count is low, you should end the round as early as possible—before your opponents draw enough lucky cards to win.

OLD-FASHIONED RUMMY (STRAIGHT RUMMY)

Number of players: Two to six.

Object: To get rid of all your cards by melding and by laying cards off onto others' melds.

The cards: A regular pack of 52 cards; aces are low.

To play: For five or six players, deal six cards each. For two, three, or four players, deal six cards or seven cards each.

Turn one card up to begin the discard pile. Starting with the player at dealer's left, either take the top discard or draw the top card from the stock. Before discarding, you may table melds or lay off cards on other melds.

The game ends when someone has melded or laid off every card from their hand. A final discard is not required. If no one can go out, and you've gone through the discard pile a second time, the hand is thrown in.

Scoring: Each hand is scored independently. Winner scores for all cards still held in players' hands, whether in melds or not. If you go rummy—go out on one play—you win double.

Tip: While melding gives your opponents chances to lay off cards, if you hold onto melds too long, someone may go out.

500 RUMMY

Number of players: Two to eight, but three to five work best.

Object: To score points for melds and to meld all your cards.

The cards: For two to four players, a regular pack of 52 cards is used. For five or more players, use two packs of 52 cards. Aces are high or low.

To play: For two players, deal ten cards each; for more players, deal seven cards each.

Melds score according to the cards they contain: High aces count 15; low aces 1; face cards 10; all others their pip value.

The use of the discard pack is unusual. In other Rummy games, the discard pile is a tight stack, with only its top card in view. Here, the discard pile is spread out so that all cards are in view.

Play starts at dealer's left, and at your turn you may take the top card from stock, or you can take any card in the discard pile—not just the top discard— as long as you use it as part of a meld. You also have to take all cards above the discard you take. This is helpful, since your goal is to meld many points.

Besides making melds, you can also lay cards off on your own or others' melds. Since you'll be tallying your melds at the end of the hand, keep layoffs on others' melds within your own melding area.

Players keep cards laid off on sequence melds nearby, for scoring later. In this case, the ♣5 and ♣6 have been laid off on another player's ♣2-♣3-♣4 sequence.

The game ends when any player "goes out"—melds or lays off every card, with or without a final discard. No further melds, plays, or discards may occur. If no player should go out, the game ends when the entire stock is exhausted.

Scoring: At the end of play, total your melded cards, then subtract the count of cards left in your hand (whether meldable or not). Record each player's score. There is no added bonus for going out.

Tips: The strategy of 500 Rummy is nearly the opposite of other Rummy games. Keep high cards longer, because they're worth more. Since a discard can be available later, you may break up a low-scoring meld, allowing you to pick up more cards later. However, be careful when doing this, because someone else may have the same idea, and you could lose your card!

SCHAFKOPF

Also spelled Schafskopf, this forerunner of Skat emphasizes skill in taking tricks. In the United States, it's often known by its translated name, Sheepshead.

———◆◆◆———

Number of players: Three. (Four or five players may sit at the table, with players taking turns sitting out.)

Ranking in order from left to right, these are Schafkopf's permanent trumps.

Object: To win at least 61 of 120 points available in tricks.

The cards: A 32-card pack, formed by omitting all 2s through 6s, is used. All queens, jacks, and diamonds are trumps. The plain suits—spades, clubs, and hearts—rank A (high)-10-K-9-8-7.

To play: The three players are called forehand (to dealer's left), middlehand, and endhand. Deal one round of three cards each, then two face-down cards—called the "skat"—that are set aside, a round of four cards, and another round of three cards, for a total of ten cards per player.

First, determine who will become the "Player" against the two others. Starting with forehand, either accept the role of Player by picking up the skat and then discarding two cards, or pass. If no one accepts, play the deal as a "Least" (see "Scoring").

No matter who is Player, forehand starts play by leading any card to the first trick. Always follow suit when able, but otherwise play any card. A trick is won by the highest trump in it, or, lacking any trumps, by the highest card of the suit led. Whoever wins a trick leads to the next until all ten tricks have been taken.

Cards count as follows:

Ace	11 points
Ten	10 points
King	4 points
Queen	3 points
Jack	2 points
7, 8, and 9	0 points

At the end of play, each side counts points taken in tricks. The Player must win at least 61 of the 120 points in play (including the two discards in the count). The Player's two opponents work together to win points and defeat the Player. Their chief strategy is to "smear" each other's tricks with high-scoring cards.

Scoring: Each player gains or loses game points as follows, based on points in play:

Points in play	Game points
61–90	2
91+ ("Schneider")	4
winning all tricks ("Schwarz")	6
31–60	-2
0–30	-4
winning no tricks	-6

When the hand is played at "Least," everyone tries to take as few points as possible. Whoever has the lowest total wins 2 game points, and a player taking

This hand represents an excellent "take." You've got quite a few high trumps, though you're missing the highest one. You haven't seen the skat yet, but you can plan already on exchanging the ♣10, which will count in your tricks later. When you get the chance to trump a plain suit, use the ◆10.

no tricks scores 4 game points. If two players tie for least, whoever did not take the most recent trick (between the two) wins the 2 game points. If all three players tie at 40 points each, endhand scores the 2 game points. If you take all the tricks, you lose 4 game points.

The game ends when someone scores 10 game points.

Tips: To help you remember the rank of queens and jacks as trumps, remember the word CaSHeD—Clubs, Spades, Hearts, Diamonds.

To accept, you almost certainly need more than your one-third share of the 14 trumps. But since you'll need to score points, it helps to have an ace or two.

Of the 120 points, 75 come from the aces, 10s, and kings of the plain suits, which have only six cards each. You can't count on everyone following even to the first lead. In fact, the Player's two discards very often create a "void" in at least one plain suit. As a defender, you may find that the way to win an ace is to be able to play it when your co-defender is winning a trick in another suit. Especially when you have very few trumps, look for chances to "smear"— to discard an ace or 10—on your side's trick.

Variation: In some games, a "Least" is played with no suit as trumps, with each suit ranked, from high to low, A-K-Q-J-10-9-8-7.

SETBACK

Setback is a quick game of trumps, filled with strategy and surprise. Also known as Pitch and Auction Pitch, it is a descendent of the Mississippi riverboat game Seven Up, where players keep track of their points using a stack of seven chips.

Number of players: Three to five is best, but two to seven may play.

Object: To score points by winning high trump, low trump, jack of trumps, and "game."

The cards: A regular pack of 52 cards is used. Aces are high.

To play: Deal six cards each, in bunches of three. Starting at dealer's left, players each have one chance to pass or bid. A "bid" is a number—one through four—and each bid must be a higher number than any earlier bid.

The high bidder—the "pitcher"—plays against everybody else. Four possible points can be won in play: "high" (the highest trump in play), "low" (the lowest trump in play), "jack" (the jack of trumps, not always in play), and "game" (the highest total of cards won in play). Aces count 4; kings 3; queens 2; jacks 1; and 10s 10.

The "pitcher" always begins play by leading a card. The suit led becomes trump. Because of this rule, you can silently bid four (the highest bid) simply by pitching a card to indicate your trump lead.

Always follow suit whenever possible. If unable to follow suit, play any card. Each trick is won by the

In a four-player game, you win the bid at "Two," grateful that you didn't have to go "Three." You need to make any 2 of the 4 points. Here, "low" and "game" are the most likely points you'll win. Careful play should clear out your opponents' trumps, leaving an open path for your ♣2 to score the "low" point, and for you to win another trick with the ♦10.

highest trump it contains or, if it contains no trump, by the highest card of the suit led.

Although the defenders work together to set back the pitcher, they keep separate piles of the tricks they've each taken, since each independently scores any points earned.

Scoring: If you make your bid, score all the points you won. If you don't make your bid, you lose—or are "set back"—the number you bid. Regardless of how the pitcher fared, defenders score their individually won points.

Whoever reaches 7 points wins the game. When two players are near 7, always tally "high" point first, followed by "low," "jack," and "game."

Tips: A bid of one by the first player usually will not end the bidding, so you can often make this bid on a questionable hand to make the other players risk a bid of at least two.

An ace is always worth a bid of one, and it will often take two points, since the player with the lowest trump may have to play it. In the unusual case where just one trump is in play, it counts as both "high" and "low."

There aren't many cards in play besides the ones you see. In a three-handed game, only 12 other cards are out, in a four-handed game, it's 18. The outcome of most deals is therefore very unpredictable. However, the fewer cards out, the less likely it is that anyone will have the cards needed to set you back. For example, your king of trump will win the "high" point in a three-handed game nearly 75 percent of the time.

For a bid of four, you'll need to have the jack and win it, so your trumps need to be very good to make this bid safely. A hand like ♥A-♥Q-♥J-♥10-♣K-♣8 is likely to win four, but the bid carries a bit of risk if another player holds the ♥K and can capture the "low" point with it or, even less likely, the point for "jack." The low trump is probably easiest for you to win when it is in another player's hand.

Variation: Some credit "low" point to the player dealt the lowest trump instead of to the one winning it, but this leads to a less interesting game.

SIXTY-SIX

A member of the Bézique family, Sixty-six is a quiet game with good interplay. The name comes from the scoring: 130 points are in the game, so to win the hand, you need more than half—you need 66 points.

———◆◆◆———

Number of players: Two.

Object: To score 66 points by trick-taking and melding K-Q "marriages."

The cards: A 24-card deck of 9s through aces is used. In every suit, cards rank A-10-K-Q-J-9.

The rank of cards in Sixty-six.

To play: Deal six cards to each player, three at a time. Turn up one card designating trumps; place it slightly under the rest of the pack.

To begin the first phase of play, nondealer leads any card and dealer plays any card. You needn't follow suit, and you may trump opponent's lead.

Each trick is won by the higher trump (if any) or else by the high card of the suit led. After each trick, both players take a new card from the stock, the winner of the trick drawing first. The winner of each trick leads to the next.

Whoever has the 9 of trumps may exchange it for the trump upcard, as long as that player has won at least one trick. However, if the 9 of trumps is the last card drawn from stock, it's not exchanged; the other player takes the upcard.

Play continues in this way until the cards have all been drawn. When only two draw cards are left, the loser of that trick takes the trump upcard.

The second phase begins after the stock is gone. Players continue to play tricks from their hands, but you must follow suit; trump or play any card if unable to follow suit.

Marriages: A "marriage" consists of the king and queen of the same suit (see "Scoring"). To claim a marriage on your turn, show it and then lead one of the cards.

Closing: Before the stock is gone, a player having the lead may announce, "The game is closed." The player then turns over the trump upcard. No more cards are drawn and the play advances to phase two. Marriages may still be declared.

Scoring:

Marriage in trumps	40
Marriage in another suit	20
Each ace taken in a trick	11
Each 10 taken in a trick	10
Each king taken in a trick	4
Each queen taken in a trick	3
Each jack taken in a trick	2

Taking the last trick scores 10 unless either player closed the game. A player reaching 66 or more scores 1 game point if opponent has 34 or more, 2 game points if opponent has 33 or less, and 3 game points should opponent be trickless. The first player to score 7 game points is the winner.

During play, a player can announce "66," terminating play. The remaining cards are not played or scored. If the player announcing 66 doesn't actually have 66, opponent scores 2 game points. Should the final tally show both players over 66, but with neither having announced it, neither scores.

Tips: Keep track of your points so you can predict when you will hit 66.

If you have the trump marriage, worth 40, you need only 26 other points. If all you need to win is a few tricks, close the game.

If you have high nontrump cards, you may want to close the game just to protect a good trick-taking hand.

SOLO

This popular trick-taking game—a cousin of Whist—gives players a chance to form occasional temporary partnerships. Since you don't ever have to change seats in this informal game, Solo is well suited to a long trip.

Number of players: Four.

Object: To win enough tricks in order to fulfill your contract.

The cards: A regular pack of 52 cards is used. Aces are high.

To play: The turn to deal passes clockwise. Deal 13 cards to each player, turning dealer's last card up to specify a trump suit. The player at dealer's left, eldest hand, acts first. Eldest hand may pass or make one of the following calls, listed in rank from low to high:

Proposal (Prop): To take eight of 13 tricks with another player as partner.

Solo: To take five of 13 tricks playing alone against the three other players.

Misère (me-ZAIR): To take no tricks, playing alone with no suit as trumps.

Abondance (Abundance): To take nine of 13 tricks, playing alone against three opponents, with a suit other than the upcard as trumps. When this is the final call, announce the trump suit before the opening lead is made.

Misère Ouverte (me-ZAIR oo-VAIRT): To take no tricks, with no suit as trumps, and with the hand exposed on the table (also called "Spread").

Abondance in Trumps (Royal Abondance): To take nine of 13 tricks, with the upcard suit as trumps.

Abondance Declared: To take all 13 tricks against the other players, naming a suit as trumps.

You may only make a call if it outranks a prior call. For example, if a player has called Misère, you cannot then call Prop or Solo.

"Prop and Cop": A player proposes by saying "I propose" or simply "Prop." Any player who has not passed may accept the proposal, as long as a higher call has not been made. If you prop and no one accepts, you may convert your call into a higher one or else throw the hand in.

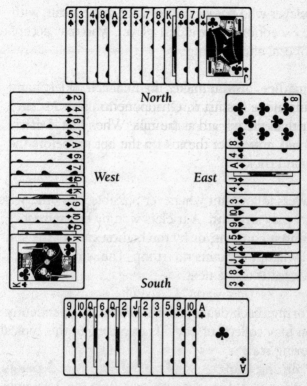

A typical Solo hand illustrating "Prop and Cop." Hearts are turned as trumps and West proposes with a good hand if joined by the right partner. North accepts on a hand without many high cards, but which will assist at hearts. East and South pass. West and North become partners for the hand. They will probably take nine or ten tricks together. West may start with the ♠A and then lead another spade, which North will trump. This is a good beginning, as the partners are using their trumps one by one.

A player who passes cannot later make a call, with the exception of the eldest player, who may accept a proposal after passing.

Regardless of who makes the final call, eldest hand leads to the first trick. One exception is at Abondance Declared, when the caller leads first. Dealer should remember to pick up the upcard before the second trick.

Players follow suit whenever possible, but otherwise may play any card. A trick is won by the highest trump it contains, or by the highest card of the suit led when it contains no trump. The winner of each trick leads to the next.

Scoring: Each deal of Solo is scored independently. You may collect, or pay off, according to this typical scoring scale:

Prop and Cop	5 points
Solo	10 points
Misère	20 points
Abondance	30 points
Misère Ouverte	30 points
Royal Abondance	40 points
Abondance Declared	60 points

Tips: Hands scoring more than Misère don't come up that often, but they are recognizable. An Abon-

dance hand might be ♣A-♣K-♣J-♣10-♣9-♣6-♦A-
♦K-♦10-♦5-♦4-♠5-♥7. A Misère Ouverte could
be ♣A-♣10-♣6-♣5-♣3-♣2-♦J-♦7-♦4-♦3-♦2-
♠4-♥3.

Most Solo hands will revolve around contracts of
Prop and Cop. As the illustrated deal shows (on
page 169), you can take tricks with low cards if your
side has the majority of trumps. In that deal, North
seized the right opportunity to "Cop." Had North
passed, East might have accepted West's prop, but
this would be a closer battle for eight tricks.

Note that for Misère, you can't have any flaw: In the
hand shown, North can be forced to win a heart
trick or a club trick; South could be made to win a
spade or a diamond at a Misère bid.

Variation: When all players pass, the hand is usually thrown in, but you may instead play a "grand,"
a no-trump contract where the winner of the final
trick loses 10 points to each other player.

SPADES

It's curious that not much has been written about this widely known, easy-to-learn trick-taking game. It's gathering new devotees from within urban America, on college campuses, and even in cyberspace!

Number of players: Four, playing as partners.

Object: To win at least the number of tricks bid by your side.

The cards: A regular pack of 52 cards is used. Aces are high.

To play: Partners sit opposite each other. Dealer deals 13 cards to each player. Spades are always trumps. There's one round of bidding, which starts at dealer's left. The first two players both bid the number of tricks—or "books"—they expect to take, while the second player in each partnership bids the total for the pair. For example, you deal, the player on your left bids four, your partner bids three, the next player bids five, and you bid seven. Your side has bid for seven tricks, your opponents have bid for five tricks.

When you are dealt many spades and a pretty good hand, you might try "10 for Two" on your own. Save bids like seven and eight for hands that need your partner's help to reach ten books.

There are several special bids that are optional in Spades.

10 for Two: A contract for ten books without a partner, with a two-to-one payoff.

Nil: A bid by the first bidder for a side for no tricks, which partner must convert to four tricks.

Blind Nil: Similar to Nil except the player may not look at the cards beforehand, though before play you and your partner may exchange one card. Your side must be down by 200 points to go for a bid of Blind Nil.

The player at dealer's left may lead any card other than a spade to the first trick. You must follow suit if able, otherwise play any card. A trick is won by the highest spade it contains or, if it contains no spade, by the highest card of the suit led.

The winner of each trick leads to the next. Until a spade has been played on a non-spade lead, you can't lead spades unless all you have in your hand are spades. When you win a book, gather it in a packet that everyone can count.

Scoring: If your side makes its bid, score the bid number times 10, plus 1 for each extra trick, called a "sandbag." If your side fails to make at least the amount bid, you lose ten times the number of tricks bid. For example, your side bids seven, and your opponents bid five. You make nine tricks, while your opponents make four. Your side scores 72 points (7×10, plus two sandbags); opponents lose 50 (their bid, times 10).

If you succeed at 10 for Two, you win 200 points, but if you fail, you lose 100. For Nil, you win 100 or lose 100 as the case may be, but for Blind Nil you win 200 at the risk of 100.

Sandbags: When your sandbags total ten, subtract 100 points from your score (don't add 10). This works as a slow penalty for "underbidding" the number of books you take. Any leftover sandbags start a new count to ten.

Play until one side reaches 500 points, or any agreed upon count.

Tips: Because of sandbags, winning extra books is no help, so be on the lookout for a situation where you have both the high card and the low card in a suit and can control winning a book or losing it. If you have ♠10-♠7, for example, and you know that the only spade remaining is an opponent's ♠8, depending upon the number of tricks you want, you can choose whether to win the ♠8 or lose it.

Variations: In some games, the ♦2 is used as an extra trump, ranking between the ace and king. Some games add a joker for an extra trump and leave out a plain-suit deuce.

An interesting alternative to start the hand is for all players to put out their lowest club (or lowest diamond, lacking clubs) for the first book. The high club in this book wins it and leads to the next trick. With the first book played this way, the strategies for bidding and play are a little different.

Some Spades games allow a generous amount of informal chat between partners before deciding on their bid. You can say nearly anything except what cards you hold.

SPITE AND MALICE

Related to Russian Bank, this game has an ebb and flow, a give and take, and many shifts of pace. Because you can often regulate how much to do on one turn, you can make plays that annoy and frustrate your opponent. It has become a curious favorite of married couples.

Number of players: Two.

Object: To be the first player to get rid of all cards from your "payoff" pile.

The cards: Two packs of 52 cards are used, plus their four jokers. Aces are low. A joker can stand for any card except an ace.

To play: Players sit across from each other with a large playing area between them. Shuffle all four jokers with one of the decks; this creates a shared draw pile, and is placed face down between the two players. Then shuffle and deal out the other deck card by card, giving each player a face-down 26-card payoff pile.

Players each turn up their top payoff card, leaving it face up on the pile. Whoever shows the lower card deals a five-card hand from the draw pile to each player. Nondealer plays first, with turns alternating thereafter.

At each turn you are required to play any aces you have in your hand or on your payoff pile into the middle of the table. An ace begins a "center stack" that is built card by card up to king. Suit and color don't matter. Each available deuce is also required to be played onto a center stack whenever possible. If there is no ace in the center, you must wait to play the 2.

In addition, you may choose to make any, all, or none of other possible plays available:

• You can play one card from your hand to begin one of your four "side stacks" (start only one side stack per turn, until you have four). These side stacks give you a chance to organize your discards.

• You can play one or more cards from your hand onto one or more of your side stacks. Each card you add to a side stack, however, must be either the same rank as the topmost card showing, or one rank below it (any 9 on any 10, for instance).

Each player can play only to his own side stacks, and only with cards from his hand. Color and suit don't matter.

- You can move the topmost card from one side stack either onto another side stack or to start a brand-new side stack (unless you already have four side stacks).
- You can play a card from your hand, your payoff pile, or your side stacks onto the center stacks. Play a 2 on an ace, a 3 on a 2, and so on upward to king. Suit and color don't matter.

Before beginning each turn, take cards from the draw pile to bring your hand back to five cards, replacing any cards you played on your last turn. Keep playing until you can't or choose not to make any further move. Just say "That's it," and your opponent takes his turn.

When a center stack is built up to the king, shuffle the cards from that stack back into the draw pile. You can wait for a few stacks to accumulate.

Bonus turns: Whenever you play all five cards from your hand in one turn, you get an extra turn. Take five new cards from the draw pile and keep playing.

When neither player can—or will—make a play, the game is blocked. In a blocked game, however, you

It's your turn. You must play ♠A to start a new center stack.
You should also play ◆9 from your payoff pile on top of the
♣8 in the center, and follow with the ♠10, ♣J from your
hand, then ♥Q-♥K. You may also begin your fourth side stack
with ◆K. Since you have a new payoff card to turn up, you
may still have plays left this turn.

must make any obvious plays your opponent re-
quests in order to keep the game moving along.

Scoring: If you play out your entire payoff pile, you
win a point for each card remaining in your opponent's payoff pile, plus a 10-point bonus. In a
blocked game, whoever has fewer payoff-pile cards

left scores the difference, with no bonus. Play to 25 points, or to any other agreed upon number.

Tips: Your immediate goal is always to reduce your payoff pile, so it is usually worth spending a joker or two to play off your current payoff card. The next card you turn up may be easy to play off.

A constant goal is to make things difficult for your opponent. For instance, try to build center stacks just past the rank of opponent's current payoff-pile card.

Try to begin your side stacks with high cards, to give yourself chances to build downward. Although you can play cards of the same rank on side stack cards, such piles are harder to empty. Sequential piles, however, play right off onto the center stacks.

Variations: Some versions let you play only one card in any turn to a side stack. Others follow the rule that layoffs in sequences must alternate between red and black cards.

TWENTY-ONE

*Don't confuse this game with the casino game of
Blackjack, also called "21." Even children can play
this easy-to-learn numbers game, and anyone can
win! It also offers a chance to practice counting
skills.*

———◆◆◆———

Number of players: Two to seven.

Object: To win as many cards as possible, without
going over 21.

The cards: A regular pack of 52 cards is used. Aces
and picture cards count 1 point each, all others
count their pip value.

To play: Deal the cards out equally, and set aside
any remaining cards. Starting at dealer's left and
continuing in a clockwise fashion, players build a
card count up to 21. As each card is played, the new
total is announced.

When you play a card that reaches 21 exactly, collect the cards in the center. However, when any card
you have would go over 21, say "Stop." The player

The count has gone 5-12-15-16-17-18. If you have a 3, you can score 21 exactly and win the cards. If you have an ace, deuce, or picture card, you can still play. Otherwise, say "Stop." The player on your right gathers in the cards, and you begin a new count.

on your right collects the cards. The player who said "Stop," begins the next count toward 21.

The hand is over when the final player gathers in the last cards.

Scoring: Players count the cards they've won, and each player's score is recorded. The first player to 50 points (or any other agreed upon total) wins.

Tip: A usual strategy for most players is to play their high-count cards early. This leads to more low cards in the later rounds, and so the center pile tends to be bigger after the first few builds to 21.

Variations: You can play this game "blind," where each player turns up a card from a pile at each turn, without knowing its value.

A similar game called Twenty-Nine is intended for partnership play. Deal 13 cards each. The player at dealer's left begins by playing any card, and players follow in turn, stating the new total with each card played. If you can't play without going past 29, you must pass. Whoever reaches 29 exactly wins the trick. The next player then begins a new count. Eight tricks are possible, although not always taken in play. The side with the most cards when no one can play exactly to 29 wins.

WAR

*Along with Old Maid, War is one of the first card
games we played as children. In practical terms, it
rarely ends with a thorough defeat.*

Number of players: Two or more.

Object: To win all the cards.

The cards: A regular pack of 52 cards is used. Aces
are high.

**When there is a tie for high card, a war is waged to deter-
mine the winner. Here, players were tied at 10, and the player
with the ♦8 is the winner of this war.**

To play: Divide the pack equally into a face-down pile for each player. At about the same time, each player turns over their top card. Whoever has the higher card wins both cards, and the process is repeated. Cards won may be placed on the bottom of your pack, or set aside until your pile runs down, at which point the cards taken must be played.

Occasionally, both players turn up cards of the same rank. This starts a "war," in which each player lays off three more cards face down, and then turns up the next card. Whoever's card is higher wins all the cards from that "war." If the cards are still tied, turn three more cards face down and then turn the next card up to determine the winner.

The game ends when one player has taken all the cards, but this can take a long time. You can try a shorter game, where you go through the cards just once or twice, and then see who has more cards. You may also decide to play until one player's hand is reduced to ten cards.

Tip: This is a game of sheer luck, so there is no advice to follow—just hope that you get most of the high cards!

Variation: For three or more players, deal the cards out as equally as possible. Turn cards as before, and when players tie for best card, each plays two more face-down cards, with the next card turned up to decide a winner. Players not in the war must also contribute their next three cards. Play continues until one player has all the cards.

WHISTLET

This game appears to be a compact form of "German Whist." Simple to play, Whistlet supplies an engaging mix of luck and skill. And you can learn to play this trick-taking game in about one minute.

———◆·◆·◆———

Number of players: Two.

Object: To win the most tricks.

The cards: A regular pack of 52 cards is used. Aces are high.

To play: Deal seven cards to each player, one at a time. Turn the next card over and place it next to the stock. The suit of this card will be trump.

Nondealer leads to the first trick. You must follow suit when you are able to; otherwise you may trump or discard. A trick is won by the higher trump in it or, if it contains no trump, by the higher card of the suit led. After each trick, both players take a new card from the stock, the winner of the trick drawing first. The winner leads to the next trick.

Each deal consists of 26 tricks. The last seven tricks are played after the stock pile is gone. (Note that the winner of the 19th trick draws the one remaining stock card: The loser of that trick takes the trump upcard.) Keep track of individual tricks each player has won.

Scoring: The player who took the greater number of tricks scores the difference between that number and the lesser number of tricks. If both players took 13 tricks, neither scores; but if one player took 15 tricks and the other took 11 tricks, the winner scores 4 points.

Tips: Even if you are void in a suit, use judgment in trumping. It may be better strategy to shed a loser by discarding it.

Your hand.

Oppenent's hand

In the last seven tricks, it will pay to have more trumps than your opponent.

Suppose hearts are trump. With the last seven tricks to go, you should play the hand at left (your hand) by leading ♥10, forcing opponent to take it with the ace. After regaining the lead, draw opponent's remaining trumps by leading a winning heart each time. Then the rest of your cards are winners, too.

The trump suit contains exactly 13 cards. If you keep count of the trumps played, you'll know in the endgame just how many trumps your opponent has.

As in most games, the better you remember the cards that have been played, the better you'll do. Keeping track of trumps and a few high cards is helpful, but if you can remember every card in the first part of the game, you'll know your opponent's last seven cards.

In the first phase of play, you may well discover opponent to be void of a suit. It may be a good risk to continue leading that suit, when your objective is to reduce your opponent's trumps. If your objective instead is to win your low trumps, then it may pay to lead a singleton, hoping to remain void in that suit later.

Variation: Play Whistlet just as above, but try to lose as many tricks as possible. When you must win a trick, use the highest card available. At the end of play, the one with fewer tricks scores the points.

SOLITAIRE GAMES

The reasons people like to play solitaire games are varied. Some games are pleasant time killers; others become intricate puzzles requiring deep concentration. The object of most solitaires is to arrange the cards in suit sequence by following certain rules. Elaborate patterns are sometimes used in laying out the cards, and for some games the pleasure of playing comes from building the array of cards. People with a mathematical bent can enjoy the type of solitaire in which you combine cards that add up to a certain amount.

Winning a solitaire game is not always a matter of luck. Some of the best games can be won quite often with careful, logical play. Other games come out so seldom that winning the game is a notable event.

ACCORDION

*Even if you're not musical, you can while away idle
moments playing the popular pastime Accordion.
Each game is quick and requires only a small space.
However, the solitaire hardly ever comes out.*

———◆❈◆———

The layout: Simply keep dealing out cards in a row.

Object: To form a single face-up pile of all the cards.

Procedure: As you deal cards into a single row, pile
cards onto other cards to the left according to two
rules of matching: (1) The two cards must be either
the same suit or the same rank, and (2) the cards
must be either next to each other or have two cards
between.

Pile matches together onto the card on the left. Then
treat any pile made as a single card. Look to see if
one move has created another. If you have no more
moves, play a new card at the end of a row.

Occasionally a newly turned card gives two possible
moves; you may make either. The game ends in a

Dealing the ♠3 gives you your first move. The ♠3 can be piled onto its match, the ♥3 (same rank). The ♠3 now matches the ♠7 (same suit) directly on its left, so the two-card pile can be moved onto the ♠7. Since no matches remain, continue by adding a new card to the end of the row.

single pile very rarely; you're doing very well to get down to just two or three piles.

Variations: Start by dealing a 13-card row, which will probably give you choices of moves to make. Before playing, you may enjoy trying to project their different results. When you've made all your moves, add new cards to the row until 13 are again showing and proceed as before.

A similar solitaire is called Royal Wedding. Start by placing the ♥Q on the top of the pack and the ♥K on the bottom. Deal out the pack one card at a time, starting with the ♥Q. As you proceed, throw out single cards and pairs of cards that stand between cards that match by suit or rank. You win the game if you wind up with just the ♥Q and ♥K, the Royal Marriage. It won't happen very often.

CALCULATION

One of the older solitaire games, Calculation is a favorite of players who like a pastime requiring skill and forethought. With a little practice in waste-heap management, you can win this one frequently.

The layout: Place any A, 2, 3, and 4 in a foundation column.

Object: To build on the four foundation cards in numerical sequences. Build on the ace by ones, on the 2 by twos, on the 3 by threes, and on the 4 by fours. Suit does not matter. The completed layout would look like the illustration on the next page.

Procedure: Turn cards from the pack one by one, building on any foundation when possible. Lay off unplayable cards into one of four waste piles, as you choose. The top card of any waste pile is always available. It's customary to spread the waste heaps downward to see the cards "buried" within each. You may go through the pack only once.

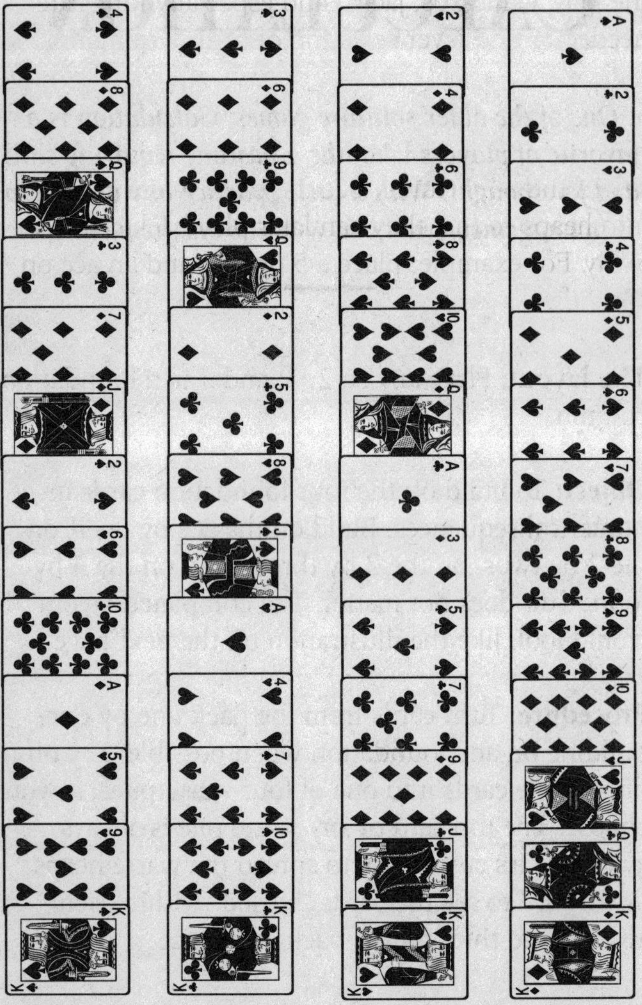

Tips: Queens, 6s, and 8s are needed fairly early in the play, while 10s, jacks, and especially kings are needed later. Clever selection of card placement in the waste heaps is essential to succeed in this game. Some players save one waste heap for the kings.

When the opportunity occurs, place waste cards into heaps so that they can later play back consecutively. For example, place a 5 on a 9, and an ace on the 5, for later playback to the 4 row.

Possible completed layout of calculation.

CANFIELD

Canfield is named after the owner of a celebrated gaming house in Sarasota Springs, New York. Mr. Canfield sold a pack of cards for $50 and paid the player $5 for every card played onto the foundation cards. Undoubtedly this venture did not lose him money.

———◆◆◆———

The layout: Deal a packet of 13 cards face down. Turn it face up and set it at the left for a reserve pile. Deal another card face up above and to the right of the reserve pile. This is the first of four foundation cards. As other cards of the same rank become available, add them onto this row.

Just beneath the foundation row, deal a row of four cards to start the tableau.

Object: To build four ascending suit sequences, each beginning with the base-number card. The suits are built around the corner: Ace follows king and deuce follows ace.

Procedure: Deal cards from the pack in threes, placing cards not used on a single face-up waste pile. The uppermost card on the waste pile remains an available card.

Add to the foundations with cards from the pack, the reserve, the tableau, or the waste heap. You may build downward sequences, alternating in color, from the tableau cards. These sequences can be built around the corner like the ascending sequences: A king can be played on an ace. You may also move an entire sequence of tableau cards onto another, creating a longer sequence, in order to clear a space. Spaces are filled with a card from the reserve pile. If the reserve pile is used up, fill open tableau spaces with available cards from the pack or waste heap.

Turn up cards from the pack in three-card bunches. The top card of a bunch is always available. If you play it, the card underneath is available. Put unused cards into a waste heap, the top card of which is available.

Turn the waste heap over each time you've gone through the pack. Keep on until the game is won or you can make no more plays.

Variation: A slight variant called Storehouse makes things a little easier for you. Always remove the four deuces in advance and use them as the foundation-row base cards. Then build on each deuce upward in suit to the ace.

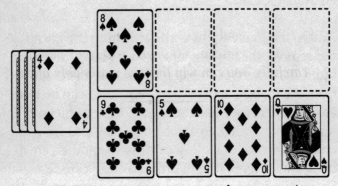

Here the first play would be to move the ♦4 onto the ♠5. Then move the ♣9 onto the ♦10. Fill any empty spaces with cards from the reserve pile.

FORTY THIEVES

This challenging solitaire is also called Napoleon at St. Helena's and Big Forty. Skillful play pays off. If you pay close attention and plan your moves carefully, you can win this one reasonably often.

❖

The layout: Shuffle two 52-card decks together. Deal out a row of ten cards face up. Overlapping them slightly, deal another row of ten cards over the first row. Continue until 40 cards have been dealt in four rows. Above these, leave room for eight foundations. See the illustrated layout on page 202.

Object: To build suit sequences on all eight aces up to the king.

Procedure: As aces are released, place them above the layout as foundations. The bottom card of each column is available and may be played in downward suit sequence onto another available card or in upward suit sequence on a foundation pile. In the illustration, once the ♥A is moved into the foundation area you can move the ♣10 onto the ♣J. Cards in the layout can be moved only one card at a time.

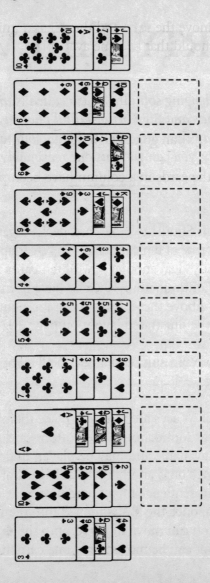

You can't move the ♣10 and the ♣J as a unit onto the ♣Q, should that become available.

Turn cards up from the stock one at a time. Cards that cannot be played to the tableau or foundations form a single waste heap, whose top card is always available. You can go through the pack only once.

When all the cards in a column have been played, fill the space left behind by any playable card.

Tips: Success is likely to rest with your ability to clear out one or more columns. With one or two spaces available for transportation, you can maneuver longer card sequences.

Variations: Some players allow tableau sequences to stack downward in alternating suit color. Although this does not keep the suits together, it offers twice as many possible plays and will increase your odds of winning.

Another way to boost your chances is to place the eight aces into the foundation row and then deal out the "40 Thieves" below.

Sample layout for Forty Thieves.

FOUR CORNERS

In this entertaining endeavor, each suit has its own "exclusive" corner. Once the layout gets started, only members may enter.

———◆◆◆———

The layout: Distribute the four aces one to each corner, as in the illustration at right. Deal four cards around each ace. In the center, leave room for the rest of the pack and a waste heap.

Object: To build each suit in sequence upon its corner ace.

Procedure: Look for deuces anywhere in the layout to place on their appropriate aces. Look for the 3s that go on the 2s, etc.

In the tableau illustrated at right, put the ♥2 and ♥3 on the ♥A, and the ♠2 on the ♠A.

Turn over cards from the pack one at a time. Discard those that can't be played into the waste heap. Refill open corner spaces by cards of the appropriate suit only (the suit which matches that corner's ace). They

Sample beginning layout for Four Corners.

may come from the pack, from the top of the waste pile, or from cards in the original layout.

As the game progresses, continue building up the four suit sequences whenever possible.

Turn the waste heap over and go through the pack again. To win, you must complete each sequence this time around.

Tips: Since you have two chances to go through the pack, it's OK to leave high cards for the second time around. Try to "park" low cards in their correct corners, as well as any intermediate cards that might soon come into play.

As spaces open up, you may have several options for filling them. Usually you should try not to fill with a high card right away, unless that opens a key low card that could get trapped in the waste heap.

When several spaces are open, with no great play to make from the waste heap, it's probably better to check out the next cards from the pack.

On the second time through, try not to bury any low card in the waste heap under a higher card of the same suit. If this happens, the game will be blocked.

GAPS

This widely known solitaire gives you a chance to put on your thinking cap. The name comes from the gaps left in the layout once play begins. Blue Moon and Spaces are among other names given to this interesting, mazelike exercise.

———◆◆◆◆◆———

The layout: Deal out the whole deck in four rows of 13 cards. Then take the four aces out of the layout and put them aside.

Object: To end up with four 12-card rows, each one should be a complete suit in sequence from 2 through king.

Procedure: You may fill any space with the next higher card to the card at the left of that space. For example, if a space lies to the right of the ♣10, take the ♣J from its present position and fill that space. This will leave a new space where the ♣J was.

Fill an empty space at the left end of a row with any deuce. A space behind a king cannot be filled. But if

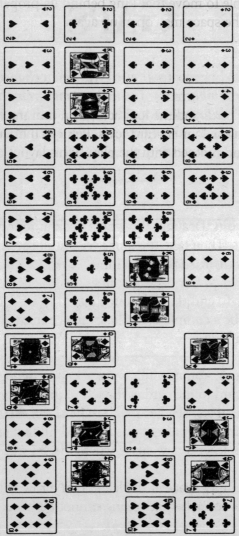

you're able to move that king behind its proper queen, the space may open up again.

When all four gaps are behind kings, card movement is blocked. Gather up all cards in the layout that aren't in their correct sequence behind deuces. Shuffle up these cards and the four aces, then deal the cards to fill out the four 13-card rows. Remove the aces as before and proceed with the play. If this layout gets stalled too, you're allowed one further redeal.

Tips: Usually three or four plays are possible at the start of a game, each opening up a series of further moves. You may see that some plays will soon lead to a useless space behind a king. To follow each line of play can be perplexing at first, but you'll get better at it after playing a few times.

It helps to identify a card you would like to move and work back to see what other cards need to move before you can move that card.

Variations: A number of players handle the redeals by omitting the aces and leaving a gap in each row

In this sample layout at left, move the ♦7 to the space to the right of the ♦6. This opens up the space for the next card in the hearts row. Moving the ♠10 to the space to the right of the ♠9 creates a block after the ♦K.

behind the last correctly positioned card. If a row has not yet been started, leave a gap at the left, for a deuce.

Gaps For Two: Gaps can be played as an interesting, though heady, competition for two. One player shuffles and deals a layout. The other then sets up an exact replica layout with another deck. There's no redeal; whoever can get more cards into proper suit sequence is the winner.

The layout at left shows the game after the unmatched cards were redealt and the aces were removed.

GOOD NEIGHBORS

Pay attention to this catchy little solitaire, also known as Monte Carlo or Weddings. It may look innocent enough, but some skill is required, since you've got many choices in the play.

———◆◆◆———

The layout: Deal four rows across of five cards each, face up.

Object: To pair off and remove all the cards in the pack.

Procedure: You may remove any pair of cards of the same rank, provided they are vertical, diagonal, or horizontal neighbors. In the layout shown at right, you'll find three such pairs: 6s, 3s, and jacks. Note that the two 8s can't be taken, due to the fact that they are not neighbors.

Fill the spaces of pairs taken by moving the remaining layout cards to the left, and then up and over to

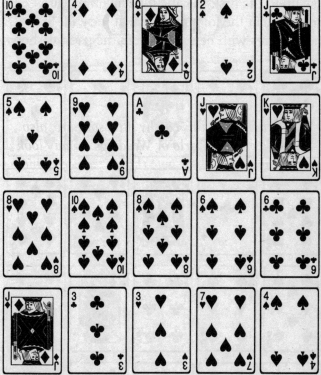

Sample layout of good neighbors.

the end of the row above. (Spaces at the right end of a row are then filled from the left-hand side of the row below it.)

For example, remove 3s and Js from the above sample layout. Move the ♠5 from the left of the second row up to the first, moving the remaining cards along so that the four spaces are at the end. Fill in those spaces with new cards from the pack as shown

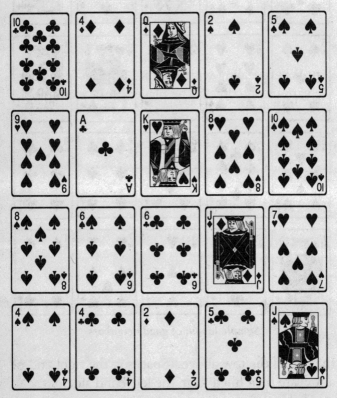

After removing the initial pairs and replacing those spaces with new cards, you are ready to look for more "good neighbors."

in the illustration on the left. Then look for more "good neighbors."

Continue removing pairs until the whole pack is taken. If at any turn the layout has no matches, the game is lost.

Tip: When dealing with a choice of plays, consider the various outcomes. The player in the example shown retained the 6s to have a sure match on the next turn.

GRANDFATHER'S CLOCK

This rousing solitaire is sure to keep you ticking. Play your cards right and bide your time—and you'll wind up with a picture-perfect finish. A nostalgic relic, Grandfather's Clock is also known as Clock Solitaire. No matter what you call it, it's "hour" favorite!

———◆◆◆———

The layout: From a double deck, select 2-6-10 of one suit, 3-7-J of another, 4-8-Q of a third suit, and 5-9-K of the fourth suit. Arrange them in numerical order as in the face of a clock, with the 6 placed at one o'clock (see diagram on page 218). These 12 cards are the foundations.

Next deal three circles of 12 cards each face up and overlapping around the outside of the clock face, as shown. These are reserves. The remaining cards form the stock.

Object: To build upward suit sequences on each foundation card, aces following kings. When the game is won, all cards have been played out and an ace sits at one o'clock, a deuce is at two o'clock, a trey at three o'clock, and so on, with a jack at 11 o'clock and a queen at 12 o'clock.

Procedure: Turn cards from the stock one by one, going through the pack just one time. Discards go into a single waste heap, whose top card is always available. On the tableau, only the outermost reserve cards are available.

A card played will release the one beneath it.

You may build onto the foundation piles from the reserves, the stock, or the waste heap. In the layout shown, build the ♦Q onto the foundation ♦J at six o'clock.

Play onto available reserve cards in downward suit sequence. In the example shown on page 218, you start by moving the ♥10 onto the ♥J, the ♣4 onto the ♣5 and both onto the ♣6. The ♥5 then released may be moved onto the ♥4 in the clock. You may move as a single unit a group of cards all connected in downward suit sequence.

When any reserve pile has fewer than three cards, fill its available slots only from the unseen stock and never from the waste heap or from other reserves.

Tips: You can win Grandfather's Clock fairly often if you make the most sensible plays and watch what's going on. Often you'll have quite a few plays and sometimes even a choice of plays between identical cards. Look to see which cards would be released by each alternative.

Sample layout of Grandfather's Clock.

KLONDIKE

Klondike is so widely known that for many people the game is synonymous with solitaire. In England the game is known as Canfield, but in the United States Canfield refers to a different solitaire. Why it has been so popular is a puzzle, since you don't end up a winner very often.

The layout: Deal a row of seven cards with the leftmost one face up and the rest face down. On top of the face-down cards, deal another row of cards, with the leftmost of these face up. Keep doing this until you have seven piles, ranging from one card on the left to seven cards on the right, with the top cards face up. The remainder of the cards form the stock.

Object: To release the four aces and build sequences in suit on them.

Procedure: As aces become available, they go into a foundation row above the layout. You can build downward sequences on the cards in the layout in alternating color only. Sequences can be moved to other piles as a unit. Top cards on the piles are available to put on the foundation piles. As cards move off their piles, turn up the card beneath. Occasionally a pile empties, opening up a vacancy. This can be filled only with a king or a sequence headed by a king.

With the tableau shown below, play the ♥A into the foundation row. Then move the ♦10 onto the ♣J, and the ♠9 onto the ♦10, and move all three cards onto the ♥Q. This releases four new cards to turn over.

When the layout has no further plays, turn cards one at a time from the stock. Play these on the foundations or layout if possible; otherwise discard into a waste heap. The top waste-heap card remains

Sample starting layout of Klondike.

available until another covers it. You may go through the stock only once.

Variations: Many favor turning the stock in bunches of three. At first this shows you only every third card, but as soon as you can use a card, then the one below it also becomes available. When the pack runs out, just turn the waste heap over and go through it in threes again. Each time through, you'll see new cards unless no cards were used in the previous round.

LUCKY FOURS

This is a "lucky" solitaire because you have a very good chance to win, yet you appear to be making one sensational play after another. For this reason, have several onlookers around. Like its relatives Shamrocks and La Belle Lucie, Lucky Fours requires plenty of playing space.

———◆◈◆———

The layout: Deal 13 four-card fans face up on the table, so that all cards are visable.

Object: To release the four aces and build complete sequences in suit up to the king.

Procedure: The top card or card sequence in any fan may be moved to the top of another group, in descending order and alternate colors. In the illustration at right, move the ♦A to a row above the fans to begin the suit foundations. Then move the ♣J to the ♦Q and move the ♣5 to the ♥6 to free up the ♠A. You can then move the ♦Q-♣J sequence to the ♠K.

The cards have been dealt. Now it's time to try and release your aces.

When a space opens up, use any available king—or sequence headed by a king—to fill the space. Continue in this manner, freeing up new cards or play off onto the foundations, until all four of the aces have been built to kings, or until the game is blocked.

Tips: Keep making sequences at the ends of fans. This will help you to unload them later on their foundations.

When you have a choice of similar plays to make, such as two red eights to go on a black 9, look ahead to what the result of either play may bring, and choose accordingly.

MISS MILLIGAN

Whoever she was, Miss Milligan has given her name to one of the most popular of the double-deck solitaire games. It's similar to Spider in that successive deals cover up the work you've done.

———◆❖◆———

The layout: Shuffle two 52-card decks together. Deal out a row of eight cards face up.

Object: To build suit sequences on the eight aces, which as they become available are placed above the row of eight cards.

Procedure: First move up any aces to the foundation row. The eight cards can be played onto each other in downward sequences of alternating colors. A sequence can be moved as a unit. Vacancies can be filled only by a king or a sequence of cards headed by a king. When you've made all the moves that you can, deal another eight cards face up over-

lapping the first row of cards and filling in any holes in the layout as you go.

After you have dealt out all the cards, a unique feature called weaving comes into play. You have the option of removing one card or sequence from the layout and setting it aside in order to play the card underneath it. If later you are able to build this card or sequence back onto the layout or onto the foundation, you can set aside another card or sequence.

Although the ♣3 is blocked on the sample layout at left, you can temporarily move ♦8-♣7-♦6-♣5 aside to play the cards underneath.

OSMOSIS

Osmosis in the outside world refers to the passing of air or liquid through a porous wall. It's not clear how this popular, luck-driven solitaire game got such a scientific name. For some mysterious reason, it's also known as Captain Kidd and Treasure Trove. You'll win at this game only a bit more often than you find buried treasure.

———————◆◆◆◆————————

The layout: Deal, face down, a column of four packets of four cards each. Turn up the top card on each. Deal the next card face up and to the right of the top packet. This card, and the three others of the same rank will be—as they show up—the four foundation bases. The remaining cards form the stock.

Object: To play off cards from the stock and tableau so as to build a chain of 13 cards in each suit. These suit chains don't need to be in order.

Procedure: Across the first row, play any cards from the tableau of the same suit as the foundation card. Overlap them enough so that all cards are seen. As

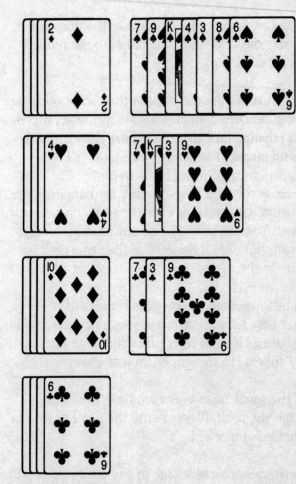

Here the base cards are 7s. Since the ♠4 has already been played in the row above, the ♥4 can be played in the hearts row. However, the ♣6 can't be played to the clubs row, because the ♥6 hasn't been played.

the top card is played from each of the piles at left, turn over the next card. The piles are not refilled when they are depleted.

Turn up cards from the pack in three-card bunches. The top card of a bunch is always available. If you play it, the card underneath is available. Unused cards go into a waste heap.

As soon as the next base-number card appears, use it to begin a second suit chain in a row underneath the first. You can now add on any card of this second suit, but only if the card of the same rank is already in the row above.

Each new row must start off with the card of the correct base number. You can join a new card to a suit chain as long as the card of the same rank already appears in the suit chain just above.

Turn the waste heap over each time you've gone through the pack. Play on until the game is won or (more likely) blocked.

Variation: Since a blockage in any tableau pile will doom the game, some players follow the variant called Peek. The four piles are dealt face up to show their contents. This permits you to see a hopeless blockage and lets you abandon the deal.

POKER SOLITAIRE

*Poker Solitaire lets you play up to 12 Poker hands
at once, and you can keep score to see how well
you're doing. This game can also be enjoyed by
two players.*

———◆◆◆◆———

The layout: Place 25 cards one by one into a face-
up grid of five columns and five rows.

Object: To arrange the 25 cards into high-scoring
five-card poker combinations.

Procedure: Shuffle the pack and turn up cards one
at a time. Place each card within the framework of
an imaginary five-by-five square of cards. Once you
place a card, you can't move it. After you've played
all 25 cards, tally your score. Total up twelve poker
hands: the five columns, the five rows, and the two
diagonals. A good score is 200.

Scoring:

Royal flush	100
Straight flush	75
Four of a kind	50
Full house	25
Flush	20
Straight	15
Three of a kind	10
Two pair	5
One pair	2

The scoring table above is the American version, which considers the likelihood of getting that hand in actual poker.

Tips: You'll increase your chances of making straights if you avoid putting an ace, 2, queen, or king in the center of the grid.

Don't plan on lots of straight flushes, but leave some chances open early in the play. Just don't wait too long to convert three cards held for a straight flush into a possible straight hand or flush hand.

Variations: Some players do not count the two diagonal hands.

As a two-player game, one player deals out the 25 cards, and the other player duplicates them with a

Royal flush   *Straight flush*   *Four of a kind*

Full house   *Flush*   *Straight*

Three of a kind   *Two pair*   *One pair*

separate deck. Each completes an independent card arrangement, in sight of each other if they wish. The location of each player's five-by-five framework should be determined at the outset. One way to assure this is to require that the first card be played in the center.

PROPELLER

Also called The Windmill, this attractive solitaire can be won often with attentive play. The name comes from the Propeller's "wings," which appear to spin around on the tableau.

———◆◈◆———

The layout: Shuffle two 52-card decks together. Take any ace from the pack and place it in the center of the layout. Place two cards face up in a line above the ace and two cards face up below it. Place two cards in a row to the ace's left and two cards to the ace's right. These eight cards are the wings. The first four kings, as they turn up, go in each of the four positions diagonal to the ace.

Object: To build four successive ace-to-king sequences in a single pile upon the center ace, and one downward king-to-ace sequence on each of the four king foundations. The sequences are built without regard to suit.

Procedure: Deal the cards from the pack one by one; either play them on one of the five foundations or discard them into a single waste pile. The top

This game of Propeller is ready to get moving.

Here is the layout from page 235 further along in the game.
You can play the ♠7 on the center ♦6. This allows you to
play the ♥8.

card of the waste pile can be played onto a foundation. The cards in the wings are also available to be played. Refill spaces in the wings with cards from either the waste pile or the stock.

You're allowed to remove a card from a king-to-ace foundation to put on the center foundation, but only once at a time. Your next play to the center has to be from the pack, the wings, or the waste pile.

Keep going until both packs play out onto the foundations or until the pack has been dealt out and the game is blocked. No redeal is allowed in this game.

THE SNAKE

This unusual solitaire is suspenseful to play and leaves a pleasing picture. Although it's very easy to win this game, you'll find it an absorbing pastime.

———◆✦◆———

The layout: Shuffle two 52-card packs together. Arrange any 13 sequential cards, beginning with a 7, into a Z-shaped tableau.

Object: To build eight-card sequences on each of the 13 foundation cards in the tableau. When successful, the complete pack will be played out, with the cards showing in value from the ace through the king.

Procedure: Deal cards up one by one and play in upward sequence on foundations whenever possible. Suit does not matter in this game. Cards turned that cannot be played are deposited in either of two waste heaps. The top card of each waste heap remains available for play and reveals the card beneath if played. No moves between waste heaps are permitted.

Tips: Skill in placing cards onto the two waste piles is what really makes a difference. For example, an 8 that is placed on a 9 in the waste pile is usually a good play, because if the 8 plays later, so can the 9. You should try to avoid placing cards in ascending order for this reason. However, since there are many playoff piles, such a play might not be fatal.

This is the Z-shaped starting layout for The Snake. Seven cards played in order on the 7, making a pile of eight, will have a top card of ace.

SPIDER

This tough solitaire appeals to those who seek a formidable challenge. To conquer it, good judgment must combine with better luck. Franklin D. Roosevelt found it his favorite solitaire. You too may find yourself caught up for quite a while in the Spider's web before winning your way out.

The layout: Shuffle together two 52-card packs. Deal a row of ten cards face down. Deal three more rows of ten cards face down on top of the first row. Deal another card to each of the first four piles. Then lay a card face up on each of the ten piles. Hold the remaining cards as a stock. The tableau should look like the illustration on page 242.

Object: To form within the layout eight suit sequences in downward order from king to ace. Sequences thus formed are taken out of the layout.

Procedure: All the action is within the tableau. You may play an upcard onto any card one rank above it, regardless of suit. You can move as a unit a sequence of cards in the same suit. Otherwise cards move singly. No card can be played onto an ace. A king or sequence headed by a king can move only into an empty space. Whenever a face-down card is uncovered, turn it up. When a pile empties, fill its space with any available card or natural sequence.

When you run out of moves, or choose to make no new ones, deal another row of ten cards face up onto the layout. First you must fill in any spaces in the layout. When the whole new row is in place, you can continue playing.

Whenever you produce an entire suit sequence, you may remove it from play. Or you may keep it in play if breaking it up can keep the game alive.

Tips: On the original deal, you want to get as many face-down cards uncovered as you can. Move cards onto cards of the same suit if possible. If such a move is not available, move top-ranking cards first. In the example shown on page 242, move the ♦6 onto the ♦7 first. You might turn up a useful card under the ♦6. If not, move the ♦10 onto the ♥J before playing the ♣9 onto the ♦10.

Each new row of ten cards is a mixed blessing—you get ten new cards to deal with, but they block all the work done so far.

Sample beginning layout for Spider.

THE SULTAN OF TURKEY

The most delightful feature of this solitaire is the pattern it creates when you win, which is more often than not. You'll be treated to a view of the Sultan— the king of hearts—surrounded by his harem of eight queens.

————◆◆◆◆————

The layout: From a double deck, remove the eight kings and one ace. Arrange them in three rows of three, with a king of hearts in the center and the ace underneath it. The cards surrounding the king of hearts are the foundations. Add a column of four cards on each side of this array. These cards are available to play on the foundations. The remaining cards form the stock.

Object: To build suit sequences from ace to queen on the seven outside kings and from deuce to queen on the ace. The central king of hearts is not built on.

Procedure: Deal cards from the stock one by one, playing them either on the foundations or to a single waste pile. The top card of the waste pile is available for play, as are the cards from the two side columns, onto the foundations. Vacancies in the columns are filled from the waste pile or the stock. You are allowed two redeals, which is usually enough to make the game come out.

A sample setup of The Sultan of Turkey.

TUT'S TOMB

Many solitaires call for adding cards together. This is a version of a widely popular solitaire called Pyramid. Here the king of spades represents King Tutankhamen of Egypt and rests atop a mighty pyramid of cards.

———❖———

The layout: Put the ♠K down first, and create a pyramid of overlapping rows as shown on the next page. The last row will have seven cards. Keep the rest of the pack as a stock.

Object: To play off all the cards in pairs that add to 13. Cards have the same value as their rank. Aces count 1, jacks 11, and queens 12. Kings count 13 and are removed from the pyramid alone.

Procedure: Remove all pairs of available cards in the layout that total 13. At the outset, only the lowest pyramid cards are free. As cards are removed, new cards become exposed above.

This game of Tut's Tomb (right) is ready to begin.

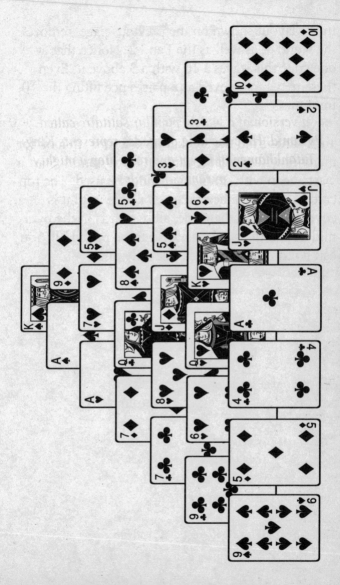

In the layout shown on the previous page, remove the 9 and 4, as well as the J and 2. Notice that at one edge this leaves a 10 with a 3 above it. Even these may be removed as a pair, since lifting the 10 frees the 3.

Turn cards from the stock, one at a time, to look for matches with available cards in the pyramid. Start a waste heap with cards that cannot be used. The top card of the waste heap stays available until it is covered. To win the game, all the cards in the pyramid and in the stock pile have to be paired off. You can go through the stock pile only once.

GLOSSARY

On the following pages, you will find all of the key words used in the card games in this book listed with their definitions. Once you learn the language, and the basics of the many enjoyable games in this book, you will be on your way to a lifetime of intriguing card play!

❖

Bella. In Klaberjass, the king and queen of trumps.

Bid. A spoken declaration to win a specified number of tricks or points; also, to make such a declaration.

Big Casino. In Casino, the ten of diamonds.

Blucher. In Nap, one of three bids to take five tricks.

Build. In Casino, to combine two or more cards so they can be taken with another card; also, the combination itself.

Canasta. In Canasta, a natural canasta consists of a meld of seven cards of the same rank. In a mixed canasta, from one to three cards are replaced by wild cards.

Contract. An agreement to win a certain number of tricks or points in a game or round.

Crib. In Cribbage, the extra hand, belonging to the dealer, formed by the players' discards.

Cutthroat. Each player playing on his or her own.

Deadwood. In Rummy games, cards in a player's hand that remain unmelded.

Deal. The act of portioning out the cards to the players; also, the period of play in the game between one deal and the next.

Declaration. A statement to fulfill a contract.

Deuce. A card of the rank of two; also called a two-spot.

Dix. In Pinochle, the lowest trump.

Draw trumps. To lead high trumps in order to deplete opponent's hand of trumps.

Draw. To take a new card or cards.

Face card. A king, queen, or jack.

Face value. The numerical value of a card.

Flush. A set of cards all of the same suit.

Follow suit. To play a card of the suit led.

Foundation. In solitaire, a starting card on which specific other cards are played.

Four of a Kind. In Poker, all four cards of the same rank.

Full house. In Poker, a hand with three of a kind and a pair.

Game. A total number of points to achieve; also, what constitutes winning or ending a game.

Gin. In Gin and Rummy games, a hand completely matched in melding sets, with no deadwood.

Going out. Playing, melding, or discarding your final card.

Hand. The cards dealt to a player; also, the period of play in the game between one deal and the next.

Jass. In Klaberjass, the jack of trump.

Kitty. A common chip-pool; also (in a few games) cards available for exchange.

Knock. In Rummy and Gin Rummy, to end play by laying down a hand that is not completely matched.

Lay off. To play one or more cards according to allowable plays.

Lead. To play the first card to a trick.

Left bower. In Euchre, the jack of the same color as the trump suit.

Little Casino. In Casino, the two of spades.

Maker. A player who takes on a specific obligation, such as to take a certain number of points or tricks, often along with the right to choose the trump suit.

Marriage. A meld consisting of the king and queen of a suit.

Match. To equate by being of the same rank (or by another criterion).

Meld. A combination of cards with scoring value, generally three or more cards in sequence in one suit or all of the same rank; also, to show or play such a combination.

Menel. In Klaberjass, the 9 of trump.

Misère. In Nap, a bid of three no trump.

Napoleon. In Nap, one of three bids to take five tricks.

No-trump (no trump). The condition when no suit is trumps in a trick-taking game.

Pair. In Poker, two cards of the same rank.

Pass. A spoken declaration not to make a bid; in Hearts, three hidden cards exchanged amongst the players.

Peg. In Cribbage, to score points.

Plain card. Any 10, 9, 8, 7, 6, 5, 4, 3, 2, or ace.

Pot. A pile of chips or counters to be collected by the winner.

Quartet. In Cribbage, four cards of the same rank.

Reserve. In solitaire, a group of cards available to be played.

Right bower. In Euchre, the jack of the trump suit.

Royal flush. In Poker, an ace-high straight flush.

Schmeiss. In Klaberjass, a proposal to either accept the upcard as trump or throw in the deal.

Sequence. Two or more cards in consecutive order.

Singleton. A holding of only one card in a suit.

Skunk. In Cribbage, to win by at least 30 points (or 60 in a game of 121).

Speculation. In 2-10-Jack, the ace of spades, which is the highest-ranking card.

Stock. The undealt cards available for future use.

Straight. In Poker, five cards in sequence but not in the same suit.

Straight flush. In Poker, five cards in sequence and in the same suit.

Table. The playing area; also, to lay down a meld on the playing area.

Tableau. In solitaire, the layout of cards on the playing surface, not including the foundations.

Talon. A portion of the pack reserved for later use during the deal.

Three of a Kind. In Poker, three cards of the same rank.

Trail. In Casino, to play a card to the table without building on or taking in other cards.

Trey. A card of the rank of three; a three-spot.

Trick. A round of cards played, one from each player's hand.

Triplet. In Cribbage, three cards of the same rank.

Trump. A suit designated to be higher-ranking than any other suit; any card in that suit. Also, to play a trump card on a trick.

Undercut. In Gin Rummy, to show a hand with deadwood counting less than or equal to the knocker's hand.

Upcard. The first card turned up after a deal, often to begin play or initiate a discard pile.

Void. A lack of a suit in a player's hand.

Wellington. In Nap, one of three bids to take five tricks.

Wild card. A card or cards, established before the game begins, that can be designated by the holder to stand for any other card (or cards).